About the Authors

T. J. Georgi was born at Niagara Falls, Ontario, raised in New Brunswick, and has lived her whole adult life in Alberta, where she met her future husband the moment she stepped off the plane. Tamela has worked at many jobs, but writing is the constant thread in her life. She writes the stories that refuse to let her sleep at night. Tamela is a world traveller and history lover who has always rooted for the underdog.

Lisa Wojna, originally from Winnipeg, Manitoba, has worked as an editor and reporter in the community newspaper industry, but now focuses on freelance projects. Her articles have appeared in magazines such as Chickadee, NeWest Review Magazine, and the Western Dairy Farmer. With her four children now grown, she has acquired two shelties that accompany her wherever she goes in search of a good story.

To William, Nellie, Eva, and Uncle Bill—
my heroes on the Other Side. –T. J. Georgi

To my husband, Gary, my children, Peter, Melissa,
Matthew, and Nathan, and my darling granddaughter, Jada—
the super ordinary heroes in my life. –Lisa Wojna

Super Ordinary Heroes

True Stories of Big-hearted Albertans

T. J. Georgi and Lisa Wojna

Cover and interior design by Cheryl Peddie / Emerge Creative
Cover image by Douglas E. Walker, Masterfile
Edited by Alex Frazer-Harrison
Copyedited by Terry McIntyre
Proofread by Ann Sullivan
Scans by ABL Imaging

A Note on the Type: The type in this book is set in Goudy. Designed by Frederic W. Goudy for American Type Founders in 1915. This font is often used in advertising, and continues to look "reassuring to our modern eyes". Source: www.linotype.com

The publisher gratefully acknowledges the support of The Canada Council for the Arts and the Department of Canadian Heritage.

Canada Council for the Arts   Conseil des Arts du Canada

We acknowledge the financial support of the Government of Canada through the Book Publishing Industry Development Program (BPIDP) for our publishing activities.

Printed in Canada by Transcontinental

10 09 08 07 06 / 5 4 3 2 1

First published in the United States in 2006 by
Fitzhenry & Whiteside
121 Harvard Avenue, Suite 2
Allston, MA 02134

Library and Archives Canada Cataloguing in Publication
Georgi, Tamela, 1957-
         Super ordinary heroes : true stories of big-hearted Albertans / T. J. Georgi and Lisa Wojna.

Includes bibliographical references.
ISBN-13: 978-1-894856-76-8
ISBN-10: 1-894856-76-7
         1. Heroes—Alberta—Biography. 2. Alberta—Biography.
I. Wojna, Lisa, 1962- II. Title.
FC3655.G46 2006   920.07123   C2006-900180-4

Fifth House Ltd.
A Fitzhenry & Whiteside Company
1511, 1800-4 St. SW
Calgary, Alberta T2S 2S5
1-800-387-9776
www.fitzhenry.ca

Contents

Acknowledgements

From Tami Georgi:

Thank you to Charlene Dobmeier for making that giant leap of faith. To my husband, Wasfi, for much more than I can ever say. And to Lisa, my long-suffering writing partner and one of the hardest-working people I know.

To the living heroes: You know who you are, although you'll never admit it. You are the reason. To the heroes who have passed from this world, like Barb Tarbox, Dr. A. J. Greenaway, Charlie and Winnie Ellis, Albert Blazey, and Clarence Smith, I hope to meet you one day.

To Brent Patterson of Louis St. Laurent School, Barb Skowronski, Tammy Beakhouse, and John Contessa, for bringing to life the memories of Barb Tarbox.

To Myrna Pearson, Walter and Betty Lindley, and Jennifer O'Brien for sharing their memories of Charlie and Winnie. To Mary Weaver, museum manager of the Rocky Mountain House Museum and one of the sweetest people on Earth, I'm forever in your debt. Thanks also to Hazel Chambers, Sandra Greer, and Valentina Lopatko.

To Lesley MacDonald of Global TV Edmonton, you made Shirley's day.

Last, but certainly not least, to the heroic editors Meaghan and Alex, and the staff at Fifth House. It really does take a village to write a book.

From Lisa Wojna:

Life sometimes happens when you least expect it. And it takes the courage and extra effort of a lot of people to make the difference between success and failure. Without the collective assistance of a number of individuals, I would have been unable to make the contribution to this wonderful collection that I have.

I owe an enormous amount of gratitude to the wonderful everyday heroes I profiled: Gordon Smith, Jude Fine, Yvonne Cardinal and her son David on behalf of Robert Cardinal, and Jeff Liberty. Their stories were beyond amazing and encouraged me personally during a very difficult year.

To Tami Georgi, who had to work extra hard on this project, I sincerely thank you. To a great editor, Alex Frazer-Harrison, thank you for your thoroughness and wonderful insights. To the team at Fifth House, especially Meaghan Craven and Charlene Dobmeier, thank you for your patience. And to you, our readers, may you be as blessed by the lives profiled in this book as we all have.

Introduction

They are everywhere.
They are your neighbours across the back fence. They are the people you work with. They are a best friend's grandparents. They are ordinary people doing extraordinary things. They are everyday heroes in Alberta.

When we started writing this book, we didn't know how many people we passed on the street every day had such incredible stories to tell. We met people who have overcome obstacles the rest of us can only imagine. Others went far beyond their responsibilities in life to make a stunning contribution to a person or to society.

Yet people constantly told us, "I'm no hero." In fact, some got downright upset for getting caught in the act of doing good. They were embarrassed and humble and most would do almost anything to shun the spotlight—and they were exactly the kind of people we wanted to write about. In a world where we can view enough human misery in a single hour of TV to last a lifetime, we need our heroes more than ever. Instead of searching for the good news tucked away on the back pages of a newspaper or the tail end of a news broadcast, we dared to bring these people out into the open—where they belong. Their simple acts of bravery and kindness often went unnoticed. But *we* noticed, and we knew we were sharing the same streets with angels.

This was not an easy book to write. How do you define a hero? First we decided to choose people who had gone above and beyond their expected roles, or people who had overcome huge obstacles and were an inspiration to the rest of us. But we found a better way of choosing heroes for this book: if they touched our hearts, we'd found our heroes.

We've also had to redefine our understanding of courage, giving, and, most of all, love. Now when we think of those words, a certain face will come to mind—one of the faces in this book. We asked ourselves, could we do what this person did? Could we run into a burning apartment to save a child? Could we spend our last days on Earth warning people about the dangers of smoking? Would we dive into a river to save a woman drowning in her car? But you don't have to risk your life to be a hero. Several of the people we interviewed reached out to change one life or make a small difference and ended up changing the world a little for all of us.

We soon realized that most of the stories had not just one, but several heroes. One act of courage is contagious. It reminds the rest of us that we just might have it in us to do the same.

It's a sacred trust to write the stories of the heroes in this book. For a brief time we were able to hold these stories in our hands and hope that we could do justice to them. There is nothing more humbling than that. Now it's time to pass them on to you.

We have been forever changed by these heroes, and we hope that you will be changed by reading their stories. And may each of us be caught in the act of doing good.

Ron Lyle, the "Bear Man" who survived a bear attack over fifty years ago. A whole town rallied to save his life. (Photo by T. J. Georgi)

Ron Lyle

Ronnie knew I would come

Ron Lyle *didn't know it when he set out on foot to bring in some horses on that rainy morning more than fifty years ago, but he would be staring down death before noon.*

It was 7 August 1952, and Ron had been a forest ranger for five years. He loved the life, even when it had been raining for days on end and he had to slog through the soggy forest in his rubber boots to find the ranger station's horses. This morning, he found himself a few miles out from the isolated forestry cabins of the Meadows station—his home for most of the year—but it might just as well have been on the other side of the planet. Up here in the foothills of the first range of the Rocky Mountains, thirty-five miles southwest of Rocky Mountain House, there was peace and silence as nature had intended—just one of the reasons why he'd chosen this life.

Ron listened for the horse bell as he walked with a pannier of oats to lure them in. When rangers let their horses loose to forage, they looped a bell around the neck of one of them, knowing that when you found one, you would find the others. Horses instinctively stay together.

Risks were part of the life out there, the price you paid for having the greatest job on Earth. Miles from civilization, rangers could encounter dangerous terrain and unpredictable wildlife at any time. Despite these dangers, Ron often didn't carry a gun, although he admitted that his rifle was his best friend at times. And even though he'd recently had one unnerving encounter with a black bear, he wasn't carrying one this day, either.

It had happened just a week before when Ron had set out with a bucket to gather some berries. Without warning, he suddenly found himself staring down a black bear in the spruce trees.

The bear growled and lunged at him. Ron ran.

"I came to a big spruce tree," he recalls. In a split second, he had to weigh his chances of survival between climbing the tree or running away. He knew his life would be decided in that moment. For reasons he'll never understand, he decided to make a run for it, and he somehow managed to escape from the bear.

That incident shook him up, but it was still not enough to make him carry a gun all the time. Now, a week later, as he listened for the horse bell, his ears picked up another sound, an all-too-familiar sound. It was the low warning growl of a bear.

Ron whirled around and saw another black bear about sixty yards away. Without a firearm, he had to make the most important decision of his life—again. He ran up a bank and this time, instead of running away, he took the second option and shimmied up the nearest tall tree. Ron only got about eight feet from the ground when he felt the tree shudder. The bear was inches below his feet.

Before Ron could react, he felt a pain like fire in his foot. Looking down, he saw the bear had torn his rubber boot and slashed his foot. Ron scrambled higher—he was now about thirty feet off the ground—but the bear just raced up the tree after him without missing a beat.

Not good, he thought. Ron braced himself into the tree and gave the beast a mighty kick.

"The bear took a swipe and missed and fell. He lost his grip on the tree," Ron remembers.

Incredibly, the bear broke its own fall by grabbing the tree trunk near the bottom. _Maybe this time_, Ron prayed, _it will just give up and go away._

Unfortunately for Ron, this bear was no quitter. It clambered right back up the tree and this time successfully hooked Ron by the foot. The bear's hold on Ron was solid and the forest ranger was literally ripped off the tree. Ron remembers falling thirty feet to the ground, and then nothing.

Ron came to with crushing pain in his neck, arms, and shoulders. A quick look around told him the bear had left—for now. But something was strange. As reality slowly filtered back, Ron realized he was no longer under the spruce tree where the bear attacked him— he was sure of that. The bear had dragged him some distance and left him hidden under the low branches of a different tree. For some reason, the bear had not killed him.

Under normal circumstances, one might count his blessings, but Ron, as an experienced ranger, knew better than anyone that the situation wasn't good. He was miles from the cabins where his assistant, Ed Weideman, and their summer student, Don Fregen, awaited his return. Ron was in more pain than he'd ever felt in his life, and he knew he was going to black out again soon. *If I do and the bear comes back . . .*

Then he noticed a trail in the tall grass. While he was unconscious, the horses must have walked right past him. He followed their trail out.

When he caught up with the horses, it was Dusty who walked over to him, curious. Of all their horses, Ron least expected Dusty to come to him. Dusty, a roan gelding, was the temperamental one found in every herd that shied away and would never come when called.

Ron knew he couldn't walk back to the cabins on his own and there was no way he could haul himself onto Dusty's back. But he might just be able to walk leaning against the horse for strength.

Ron took his belt off and pulled it through the bell strap around Dusty's neck. They set off for the cabins with Ron barely able to hang onto the horse as the pain shot through him.

But Dusty wasn't a completely reformed horse. Already he seemed to be regretting his humanitarian act and wanted to return to the other horses. Ron had to constantly steer him back towards the cabins. The struggle was draining him of what little strength he had left. But it was a struggle he had to win.

Ed Weideman couldn't believe his eyes when he saw the station's cantankerous horse, Dusty, walk slowly into camp with something— or was it someone?—attached to his side. Of course, it was Ron, who with Dusty's reluctant support had made it the two miles back to camp.

The story could end here. But in fact the story was just beginning. Ron needed a doctor, fast, and the nearest doctor was in Rocky Mountain House, thirty-five miles away across some of the most rugged and isolated country in Canada. There was no road out of the Meadows camp; the rangers had to cross the powerful North Saskatchewan River on a flimsy cable car each time they had to go out for groceries or anything else.

Ed radioed Ben Shantz at the Shunda ranger station, fifteen miles to the north. Ben quickly relayed the message to Rocky Mountain House, which was the forestry headquarters for the region.

The news ripped through the town. They knew a ranger had been badly mauled by a bear, and they also knew that the odds of getting him out or of getting a doctor out there in time to save him were slim to none.

Word reached Don MacDonald, one of Ron's fellow rangers. By now it was 6 PM, about six hours since the bear attack, and from what he had heard of the man's injuries, Don knew time was running out for Ron Lyle.

Don rushed to the Mountview Hotel where Dr. A. J. Greenaway was having his supper. He gave the doctor few options and Dr. Greenaway soon found himself in a waiting forestry truck.

It wasn't the first time Dr. Greenaway had been taken away from his supper by an emergency. In the twenty years he'd been in the town, there had been plenty of missed meals. As the town's only doctor, he was well known to local residents.

"He liked to visit and he always had time for you no matter where you saw him," Hazel Chambers, a long-time resident and former patient, remembers. "He never walked—he ran. You know that bent-over, fast walk? You never saw him sauntering around. He always had somewhere to go in a hurry.

"He was like the mail. Weather didn't stop him. He went regard-less."

Dr. Greenaway was now almost seventy—with many adventures behind him in a career in Rocky Mountain House that dated back to the Great Depression of the 1930s. He attended patients in raging blizzards and once made a perilous journey by car across an ice-covered river in order to deliver a baby. But he was about to take on one of the biggest challenges of his career.

He braced himself in the forestry truck as Don MacDonald burned rubber for the North Saskatchewan River crossing at Saunders, a small mining town on the way to the Meadows forestry cabins. Once they got to Saunders, however, they discovered that the ferry wasn't operating due to recent heavy rains and swift-flowing water in the river, and in those pre-cell phone days there was no way Don could have known the ferry was out until he got there. There was no choice but to use the flimsy cable car or "basket" that had to be hand-cranked over the churning river via a couple of pulley wheels. With only one man sitting on the tiny platform with a load of groceries, it was a dangerous ride that almost dipped the person into the hazardous water below.

And now, Don MacDonald had to make the trip with two men—himself working the crank and Dr. Greenaway as a passenger. With the elderly doctor wrapped in a blanket on the platform, Don got on, braced the doctor between his knees, and set off.

Dr. Greenaway must have been thinking about how they were going to get Ron Lyle out of this predicament. If it was this difficult just getting a doctor out to the remote location, how on Earth were they going to get Ron to the hospital?

After the nerve-wracking trip across the river, the two men set out on foot for the cabins and soon linked up with Ed Weideman, who came to meet them riding a tractor. The trail had become waterlogged from the recent rains and the tractor got stuck, still seven miles away from Ron's position. To make things worse, Dr. Greenaway was beginning to show serious signs of fatigue.

Don ran on ahead to the station and grabbed a horse to ride back for the doctor. It was none other than Dusty, the same horse that had reluctantly saved Ron's life.

By the time Don and Dusty found Ed and Dr. Greenaway, they'd left the tractor behind and continued on foot. But they were still three miles from the cabins. Dr. Greenaway got on Dusty and they made it to the cabin by 2 AM. It had now been fourteen hours since the bear attack.

What the doctor found when he finally reached Ron Lyle was devastating. Although the slashes from the bear were bad enough, the fall from the tree had crushed some of Ron's vertebrae. There was no way Ron would survive the kind of journey the doctor and Don had just made. His only hope was to be airlifted.

The rangers got on the radio and frantic messages sailed back and forth. Dr. Greenaway tried to stabilize Ron while the rangers made plans. The next morning, a small plane was dispatched from Edmonton, but as soon as the pilot saw the "runway"—in reality a tiny hay field bordered by huge trees—he turned his plane around and went home.

The men looking after Ron watched the plane leave with sinking hearts. If their friend was to be rescued, it would take a miracle. That, or one crazy pilot.

The rangers relayed the problem back to Rocky Mountain House. Someone recalled the exploits of a bush pilot, a man who'd been an RCAF flying instructor during the Second World War, who was now working as an auto dealer in Olds. A call was made and, with ranger Harry Edgecombe of Clearwater station beside him as a guide, pilot Mel Cipperley was soon in the air.

Meanwhile, the rescue team back at Meadows station had work to do. They set about cutting down trees to make the landing strip longer; even Dr. Greenaway was pressed into service. Ron was mostly awake during this time, but in great pain and getting weaker by the minute, and the doctor and rangers feared he wouldn't make it if the next pilot got cold feet about landing there.

Mel had to fight the treacherous wind currents of the Rocky Mountains just to reach the Meadows station. He found the makeshift runway and landed, but damp hay got caught up in the landing gear. Mel jumped out and told the rangers they'd have to clear the hay off the runway if he was ever going to take off.

Since most of the horses were still at large near the attack site, the men caught the one horse available—Dusty—and teamed him up in harness with Don MacDonald to clear the hay. The horse, never a willing participant, balked at the arrangement but finally got the job done. Dr. Greenaway, Ed, and Harry Edgecombe set off with crosscut saws to cut the larger trees at the end of the field. Finally, Mel was satisfied that with a little breeze and a whole mountain of luck, he'd be able to take off.

But by evening there was still no wind and Mel could not take off safely without it. Dr. Greenaway knew that Ron wasn't likely to survive until morning. They had to get him out now, before nightfall.

Mel agreed but insisted on first attempting the dangerous takeoff alone. The "runway" the men had created was tiny and surrounded by very tall trees. Very few planes—or pilots—could climb such a steep grade over the trees. You would need great speed, but how could you do that when the runway was so short, offering no room to gather momentum?

"If I crash there'll be only one man hurt. Lyle couldn't take any more of that kind of punishment," Mel told the others.

With that, the pilot who'd survived the Second World War and countless bush flights got ready to take off. The team addressed the problem of the plane being able to generate enough speed by holding the back of the plane down as Mel gunned the engine. At his signal, the men let go of the plane, which had built up enough speed to shudder into a steep climb. He cleared the trees! The men on the ground began to breathe again.

Mel circled and landed again. Sure, he could do it alone, but a takeoff with the weight of two men was another matter. The plane was stripped of every non-essential item, and even the extra fuel was siphoned off. Mel would have just enough to make it to Rocky Mountain House, which at least had a decent landing strip, though he'd have to get there before nightfall because the runway wasn't lit.

The men strapped Ron into the plane. As Mel raced the throttle for a head start over the trees, they once again had to physically hold back the plane. Once the engine was roaring at full throttle they let the plane go and it fired down the hay field, then lifted its nose up to the trees. Everyone on the field held their breath. But the fragile plane shot over the trees and sped onward to Rocky Mountain House.

Mel wasn't able to hear the cheers from the ground. He had other things to think about. He looked over at his frail passenger and had to wonder what was waiting for them. They'd just survived a near-impossible takeoff—one for the history books. But now, night was falling. This made a grim scenario even grimmer. How was he even going to *see* the runway in Rocky Mountain House let alone land on it? But he certainly couldn't turn around and go back, so he'd have to soldier on and hope his experience and instincts served him well.

Soon, he spotted the lights of the town, and over there—what was *that?*

In the darkness, Mel saw two rows of lights, right where the runway should be! The people of Rocky Mountain House had raced to the rescue, lining up every car and truck along the runway and turning on their headlights to light the way home for Mel and Ron.

Mel made one pass and then landed. Ron was whisked off to the local hospital where he would remain for the next two months. But he had survived.

More than fifty years later, Ron Lyle is happily retired in Calgary with his wife, Fran, whom he married in 1967. They adopted two children, a boy and a girl.

Although his patient would be alive and well half a century after the bear attack, Dr. Greenaway died of heart failure only a month after the dramatic rescue.

"He was a good man," Ron says. "I was sorry when he passed away. I was in the hospital at the time."

In spite of the attack, Ron still loved the life of a ranger and went back to it after he recovered. He still didn't like to carry a rifle but he decided to start making it a habit. And he would have to face more bears in his career. Once he was alone with his dog when a bear arrived and made it clear that it wanted the dog. Ron shielded his pet behind him and tried to stare the bear down.

"Some of them would look at me and refuse to run," he says. "It was kind of scary because you knew then what they *could* do to you."

Ron maintained a healthy respect for bears and, despite the occasional encounter, was fortunate enough not to suffer another attack like the one he endured in 1952.

Ron retired in 1978 after thirty-one years of service. Despite the dangers, most of his memories are pleasant. He would often go riding with his feisty little Pomeranian, Tiny, in the saddle in front of him. She would jump off to chase a bird in the undergrowth, but she never caught one. He watched for years as the same cow moose would return to the Meadows area to have her calf. There truly wasn't any life like it. Ron would go on to help his fellow rangers out of some tight situations of their own, and they remained friends long after he retired.

But what haunts him still is the black bear he met the week *before* the attack that nearly killed him all those years ago. Today he sees that first encounter as a kind of test, maybe a premonition.

"Afterwards I thought of that as a sort of warning," to do the right thing, he says.

But he didn't heed the warning. He didn't run. He climbed the tree instead. You don't think of that, he says, when there's a large, angry bear at your heels.

While he was in the hospital, Ron asked Ed Weideman to return to the site of the attack to retrieve his ranger's hat. Ed found the torn pannier of oats, a horse's bit, and Ron's hat and badge. And he found something else. Not twelve feet from the tree where Ron was attacked lay a decayed deer carcass.

Ed figured that the bear had been near his cached deer meat when Ron ran right toward it in his efforts to escape. The bear was likely protecting the meat from Ron when it ran after him. As it had done with the deer, the bear dragged Ron to a tree and hid him under the bottom branches. As it did with the deer, the bear would almost certainly have returned for Ron.

Ron became famous for the attack and his survival.

"I was called the Bear Man for many years," he says.

The news hit the media and even Dr. Greenaway's son Allie, who was also a doctor and studying in New York at the time, heard about it. It would become the biggest story of his father's life.

Allie asked his father why he made this insane house call at his age.

"Because Ronnie knew I would come," was the simple reply.

Ron temporarily lost his voice in the hospital from delayed shock. His back throbbed constantly for many months. Five decades later, he still experiences some pain when he tries to raise his right arm above the shoulder, a lingering reminder of the day he almost died.

Today one of the Meadows station cabins Ron used is now located outside the Rocky Mountain House museum.

Ron Lyle, himself a hero for refusing to give up after a horrific attack, survived thanks to a whole cast of unlikely characters, including a maverick ranger who wouldn't take no for an answer, a daring bush pilot turned car dealer, a dedicated sixty-nine-year-old doctor, and one very stubborn horse named Dusty.

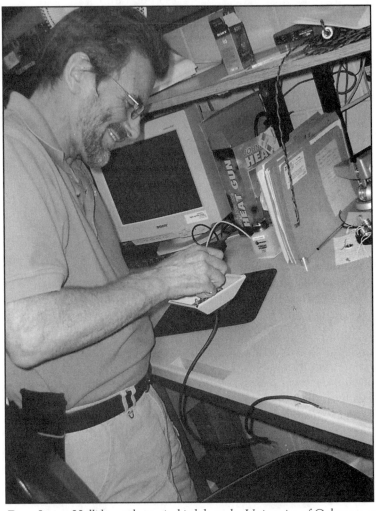

Dave Irvine-Halliday at home in his lab at the University of Calgary—a humble scholar with a very big dream. (Photo by T. J. Georgi)

Dave Irvine-Halliday

Lighting up the world

Sometimes *a life can change at the speed of light.*

In 1997, Dr. Dave Irvine-Halliday, a professor at the University of Calgary, was on sabbatical in Nepal. After spending three weeks at the Institute of Engineering at Tribhuvan University in Kathmandu, helping that school to set up a third-year electrical communications lab, Dave packed his bags and got ready to go home. Then, unexpectedly, he was asked to stay awhile longer to teach a graduate course in fibre optics. Ultimately, he would find himself spending two months in Nepal.

Dave couldn't really complain about spending extra time in the rugged Asian country. As an avid mountaineer, there was no question about what he'd do with his extra time in Nepal. He'd read about the Himalayas for years and now had an invaluable opportunity to experience them first-hand. He pondered which of the two trekking routes he would take—to the Mount Everest base camp, or along the longer Annapurna Circuit.

Dave decided on the longer and possibly more scenic Annapurna route and hired a Nepalese guide named Babu Ram Rimal to help him on the two-week-long hike. Along the three-hundred-kilometre route they followed ancient paths and passed through many villages where Babu would stop and introduce Dave to any people he knew.

In one village, an older couple welcomed Dave and Babu warmly and invited them into their home. Inside, the house was cold and dark and Dave's eyes stung from the smoke of a small fire.

"I couldn't see anyone," Dave recalls. "You just pointed your head towards the voices."

It was a sign of things to come.

In North America, we take so many things for granted. Virtually anywhere in our part of the world, once night falls we need only flip a switch and we have as much light as we need to work by, to read by, and to play by. But many of the world's people live in darkness once the sun goes down. When Canadian astronaut Roberta Bondar orbited the Earth in January 1992, she noticed something startling. Observing the planet at night, she could easily spot areas in the developed world by the sparkling diamonds of light—but in the more undeveloped regions, darkness reigned supreme.

"At night there is no distinction between land and sea except for these lacy displays of light, which are not the brilliant neon colours that we see on the ground but a yellowish-white monotone," Bondar wrote in her book, *Touching the Earth*. "The intricate network of lights in the populous industrialized areas of North America, Europe, and Japan contrasts with the more extensive areas of the world that, with little or no power, are bathed in darkness."

According to the World Bank, a third of the world's population has no access to electricity and the vast majority live in remote villages in developing countries. Kerosene is the fuel of choice to light and heat most of the homes in Nepal and the Third World, but it's expensive, hard to get, and dangerous. People—mostly women—trek for miles over the mountains to reach a trading place where they can obtain the vital fuel, and they are at the mercy of local suppliers who can raise the price on a whim.

It was a few days after his visit with the elderly couple that Dave Irvine-Halliday's life changed forever. In another village, he and Babu came upon a stone school. There was no glass in the windows and Dave poked his head inside. He was amazed at what he saw—or, rather, at what he *couldn't* see. Even though it was broad daylight outside, there was virtually no light illuminating the classroom.

Having been both a professor and a dad for many years, Dave wondered how the kids could see to read their lessons. Come to think of it, how could they see to do their homework at night?

Dave knew better than anyone the power of education to change a life. He grew up in Scotland from humble beginnings, being born in Perth and raised in Dundee. Not a single member of his elementary class went on to higher learning, but he did, earning an undergraduate honours degree in electrical engineering at the University of Abertay in Dundee, and later his Master of Science and Ph.D. at the University of Aberdeen. He moved to Canada in 1970 where he became a senior engineer for Alberta Government Telephones (now Telus). In 1980, he moved into teaching full-time as a lecturer for the department of electrical engineering at Victoria University of Technology in Melbourne, Australia. In February 1983, he returned to Canada to become associate professor at the department of electrical and computer engineering at the University of Calgary.

"What I can't tell you is why," Dave says of his love of learning, but he took to it from an early age. And that's what the kids in this Nepalese village needed, he thought in 1997—a chance at a better life that only education could give. But how were they going to get it when they couldn't even see to read their school books?

It occurred to him that there had to be a better way to light homes and schools. And if anyone could develop an inexpensive and efficient way to do it, it was this humble scholar with the boundless energy. Even before hopping on to the long flight back to Canada, Dave was already making plans.

Back at the University of Calgary, Dave went to his lab and considered the challenge. At first, he was thinking about those kids in Nepal, but then it occurred to him that if he could design something that could work in any isolated place, the idea could work in other countries.

Dave knew he had to take a different approach from what had been done before with similar projects aimed at providing light to underdeveloped regions. Merely giving people battery-operated lights didn't work. Batteries were expensive, and when they died, they were thrown away, creating environmental waste. Dave estimated that more than three hundred million conventional batteries were being thrown away in Nepal alone each year. And it wasn't as if most people could easily go down to the local grocery store and buy new batteries.

No, the kind of light that was needed had to be bright enough to read by and be powered by a renewable, affordable source of energy. He immediately thought of light-emitting diode (LED) lights. Most people are familiar with LED lighting and may not even know it. It's the little light on the front of your DVD player saying the power is on, the red light that blinks when your cordless phone needs to be recharged, and it creates the ghostly glow of digital numbers on a clock radio. LED lights are very energy efficient.

Dave immediately realized he had a problem. He had only ever seen these lights commercially available in colours, not white, because LEDs were not at the time considered to be a viable source of illumination beyond lighting up indicators or clock numbers and the like. You could easily find LEDs in red, blue, green, and yellow—just not in white, which is what Dave needed for effective lighting. But if he could find a sufficient quantity, he thought, white LED lights could be the answer to lighting up homes in Nepal and elsewhere.

After a year of work in his lab, he came up with a prototype system, but he was disappointed.

"You could barely see it, let alone read by it," he remembers. But scientists and inventors have to accept failure as a part of experimentation, so Dave regrouped and started considering a Plan B.

While doing some research on the problem, Dave discovered he was trying to reinvent the wheel. A Japanese company called Nichia had already developed white LEDs. Dave ordered a batch that same day.

When he and lab technician John Shelley received the package of LEDs a few days later, they rushed to the lab to test them. After hooking one up to a power source, they turned off all the lights in the room and waited while their eyes adjusted to the darkness. Then Dave flicked the switch.

"Good God," Dave exclaims. "[We realized] a child could read from [the light of] a single diode."

If a single LED could light up a page and then some, then half a dozen of the tiny lights were enough to make a lamp that could light an entire room. Best of all, the researchers soon discovered the lights could easily be recharged with a solar panel or a pedal-powered generator. Villagers would no longer have to trek countless miles in search of volatile kerosene or put up with replacing batteries.

Dave knew that it was one thing to create the LED lamps, but it was another to get them out to the people who needed them. At first he was alone with a giant dream and limited resources to carry it out.

But, in a great leap of faith, Dave's wife, Jenny (who shared his dream), suggested they use all the personal credit available to them to produce the necessary lights and equipment themselves. Dave got to work constructing the systems, and by May 1999 he was ready. Dave and Jenny took experimental lamps made with four hundred of the new "WLED" (white LED) lights to numerous villages throughout Nepal to see if the villagers found them acceptable.

When Dave remembers the reaction of the first people to see the lights, the tough mountain climber gets teary.

"The acceptance of the wee WLED lamps by the villagers was far beyond even our wildest expectations," he says in his Scottish accent. "It's choke-up time."

Such was the response to the WLED systems that Dave knew right away that his Nepal Light Project was only the beginning. In 2001, Dave joined Ken Robertson, Roy Moore, and his university secretary, Pauline Cummings, to establish the Light Up the World Foundation (LUTW) under the auspices of the University of Calgary. By 2005, it would grow into an international humanitarian organization.

LUTW's original goal was to "light up the lives" of a million people around the world by 2005, says Dave. But soon their goal became even more ambitious—to reach the approximately two billion people around the world who don't have access to adequate lighting. A gargantuan task perhaps, but Confucius said it is better to light one candle than to curse the darkness.

LUTW is well on its way to fulfilling its goal. As of 2005, people in dozens of countries have received Dave's WLED systems, including Afghanistan, Dominican Republic, Ecuador, Guatemala, India, Nepal, Mexico, Pakistan, the Philippines, Peru, and Sri Lanka.

With lightning speed, awards and accolades came rushing in. In October 2002, Dave received the Rolex Award for Enterprise in Tokyo. The Rolex Award supports innovative projects that advance human knowledge and well-being.

One of the selection committee members for the award was Dr. Anatoly Sagalevitch, a scientist specializing in deep-sea diving who also appeared in James Cameron's movie *Titanic*. He said of Dave: "In my childhood village outside Moscow, we had no electricity. In the evenings my brother and I tried to read using a kerosene lamp or a candle. My grandmother would get angry because she wanted to save every penny for food. With his noble action, David Irvine-Halliday will bring paradise to many houses and to thousands of children's hearts."

The prize gave LUTW a much-needed boost of $100,000 US. But there was more to come. A month later, Dave and LUTW received the Tech Museum's Knight Rider Equality Award and $50,000 US. This award honours innovators and "dreamers" who improve the human condition through technology.

Dave was also named *Reader's Digest's* Canadian Hero of the Year for 2004.

"Dave Irvine-Halliday's commitment to finding a light source for the people of Nepal—and the rest of the Third World—is truly remarkable," said *Reader's Digest* senior editor Ron Starr. "We were impressed with the professor's ability to develop, lead and deliver on an idea that has significantly improved the quality of life in many communities around the globe."

Dave's acceptance speech, however, was typically modest.

"As Canadian Hero of the Year, I hope to draw more attention to the foundation and get the help we need to truly light up the world," he said.

Dave had no idea, on that day back in 1997 when he stuck his head inside a remote schoolhouse just how many hats he'd have to wear on his journey. Clearly, lighting up the world is not just a matter of inventing a better lamp.

To him, the extensive media coverage he and his project received were simply a means to an end—that being the goal of providing millions of lights to the world's poor. He was filmed by *National*

Geographic, CNN, and the Discovery Channel. Several supporters even tried to interest American talk show superstar Oprah Winfrey in profiling the project.

Dave realizes he has become a bit of a celebrity and, like many others who find themselves thrust into the limelight, is uncomfortable with the title. He often gets a little upset when the spotlight focuses only on him and not on the others who helped establish the foundation in 2001.

"I can't change history, I'm the founder [of LUTW]," he says. "But I want other people to be recognized as well."

But it's human nature to identify with a person, not an organization. It was Dave's passion that started it all that fateful day in the Himalayas, and it's his passion that continues to draw people to his cause. If this is what it takes to light up the world, then the shy professor must reluctantly accept it.

But like all good scientists, Dave Irvine-Halliday is far more at home in his lab than behind a podium accepting awards. Students and visitors to his lab are often treated to a demonstration of the WLED system.

A WLED lamp looks for all the world like a kid's Lite-Brite, but this is no toy. The lamp is inside a small shade and made up of a snowflake pattern of tiny white LED bulbs, usually fifteen to a lamp. The light is so bright it can hurt your eyes if you stare into it directly—it's ten to twenty times stronger than an ordinary incandescent bulb. These lights are incredibly energy efficient: an entire village can be illuminated using less energy than a single hundred-watt bulb requires. Unlike a household light bulb, which can become hot enough to burn one's fingers, LED lights are only slightly warm to the touch. And, unlike standard bulbs that burn out and need replacing—usually late at night when you don't have a spare bulb handy—LED lights can last as long as twenty years without needing replacement.

In his lab, Dave demonstrates the simple pedal generator connected to a motor he bought at a Calgary auto shop. The generator has a spinning shaft that was not doing anything useful with regards to the WLED system. The practical Scot couldn't bear to see that energy wasted, so he designed a way to use this extra feature for spinning wool or sharpening knives.

The system is inexpensive, too. On average, Dave says, a villager can expect to pay $50 to $70 US a year for a few years for their lighting system, as opposed to around $30 to $120 US for kerosene every single year for the rest of their lives. Once the LED lights are paid for in a few years, that money can then be put to other uses. In Nepal the average annual income for a villager is just $200 US.

Also, by no longer having to rely on kerosene, people are no longer at risk from any of the inherent dangers of the fuel.

Kerosene lamps are easily tipped over, causing house fires and many deaths. LUTW's website states that approximately forty per cent of burns in Sri Lanka each year are caused by kerosene lamps breaking due to heat fracture or accident. Homes and entire villages have been known to burn to the ground when a lamp tips over. Of those who aren't killed, many thousands are maimed for life each year, suffering blindness and loss of limbs. In 1998, some 282,000 deaths worldwide were blamed on mishaps involving kerosene lamps and candles. Of these victims, ninety-six per cent were in developing nations.

There are other hazards associated with kerosene. The World Bank estimates that breathing kerosene fumes on a regular basis is equivalent to smoking two packs of cigarettes a day. Two-thirds of female adult lung cancer victims in developing nations are non-smokers.

In addition, kerosene is not considered an efficient source of light. Kids can't see their school books from the light of a kerosene lamp unless they sit almost on top of the flame, further breathing in the fumes.

And widespread kerosene use also has potentially global consequences.

Lawrence Berkeley National Laboratories has stated the primary source of greenhouse gas emissions in the developing world comes from dirty, hazardous fuel-based sources, such as kerosene for lighting. It says the only real way to meet the increasing lighting energy demands is to replace this fuel-based lighting with solid state lighting systems, such as the LUTW's LED lights. Dave Irvine-Halliday's vision of providing lights to millions could, in the long term, also provide untold benefit to the environment.

The LUTW organization and Dave Irvine-Halliday never intended to be the sole provider of LED lighting systems—with a goal to light up the world for two billion people, it simply did not have the resources to make this a reality. As word spread of the success of the systems in Nepal and elsewhere, other organizations picked up the cause.

In the Dominican Republic, for example, Add Your Light (AYL), a registered charity, partnered with LUTW to provide light to 187 homes (560 lights) in the El Hato region. AYL is run by Dr. Jan Tollefson, a public health doctor who has become involved in many projects since she started volunteering at an orphanage there in the 1990s.

In Afghanistan, 118 homes were lit by two Canadian members of the International Assistance Mission–Canadian Development Program. The rural community of Karez Kalan in the Mazar-e-Sharif region was selected for the lighting project in order to promote education and literacy training. By day, people worked hard to make a living, and the only time to hold classes was at night. They needed lighting for the classrooms.

LUTW also worked with several groups in the Philippines, including the World Wildlife Fund (WWF). The WWF began a pilot project to light twenty-five homes and at one point considered expanding this to reach more homes. Its rationale: people use forest timber for lighting, which destroys habitat and affects watersheds, but the LED system provides an alternative to wood.

Luxtreks, an LUTW affiliate based in Canmore, Alberta, lit 253 homes in northern Pakistan during the fall of 2003 and also planned to build a school in the region. Other Luxtreks projects took place in a Nepalese village in 2000, two villages in Bolivia were completed by September 2002, a Guatemala community in April–May 2003, Bolivia and Peru in May 2004, and Tanzania in October–November 2004, with more projects planned for the future.

In 2003, Dave Irvine-Halliday and one of his graduate students, Rodolfo Peon, travelled to Mexico to give a presentation on WLED lighting. They met members of the Marist Brothers, a Catholic order that had worked with the people of northern Mexico for thirty years. A deal was struck, and the Marists went on to light one hundred homes using LUTW's systems.

Still more people were inspired by Dave Irvine-Halliday's work. David Wiwchar's project in Costa Rica shows that you don't have to be involved with a large organization to make a difference. Wiwchar, a grade ten and eleven science teacher at Lasalle Secondary School in Sudbury, Ontario, read about LUTW in *Canadian Geographic* and immediately thought of the families he and his family had once visited in remote regions of Costa Rica. The student council at David's school bought the first five lighting systems and planned to raise funds for another thirty a year. David's children hiked into isolated areas of Costa Rica to help him deliver the lights, and he plans to take a group of students from his school on a future trip.

"We hope to keep up our yearly shipment [of lighting systems] until the project becomes self-sustaining with the purchase of systems out of the payments made by recipients," says Wiwchar.

Another unique project is the Wechiau Lighting Initiative, a partnership between Canadian Hydro Developers Inc., LUTW, and the Calgary Zoo Conservation Fund. It was set up to provide solar-powered solid state lighting units to ten thousand people living near the Wechiau Community Hippo Sanctuary in the West African nation of Ghana. The sanctuary consists of seventeen villages, seven schools, and two health clinics on the Black Volta River. It has one of only two remaining hippopotamus populations in West Africa.

Donations to LUTW provided the initial funds for people in the Third World to set up the lighting systems, but the foundation encouraged these same people to set up and operate their own companies to sustain the lighting. The women who used to travel long distances for kerosene started their own battery-charging businesses for the LED lights. As LUTW reached people around the world, more countries in Asia, Africa, and South America began asking for the lights.

As time went on, Dave learned that WLED lighting changed people's lives in ways he couldn't begin to imagine. When he was delivering the system to a village in Mexico, a doctor approached him and said he could have used the lights three days earlier when he had to deliver twins in total darkness. In Nepal, where a typical household is shared by multiple generations and the family's animals, old people are constantly in danger of tripping over something or someone in the dark. One old man in the Himalayas said he was a prisoner in his own home before the lights were installed.

Dave experienced a touching moment during a trip to Sri Lanka recently. He had gone out to dinner with friends, and they were carefully making their way back through the jungle when he saw a light through the trees and called out, "Hey, that's one of our lights!"

Sure enough, they saw the unmistakable glow of a white LED. Curious, they went up to the house and were invited inside. There, Dave and his friend Lalith Seneviratne saw a group of children sleeping on their mats on the floor. The father explained that, in the darkness, snakes would slip under the door and into the house. The children couldn't get to sleep knowing this. But Dave's lights scared the snakes away, and the children could sleep. Dave was told that snakebites were the number one cause of death in Sri Lanka. The father said that this had been the first night in the children's lives that they had been able to read at night.

The aftermath of the December 2004 tsunami that devastated Sri Lanka and other countries around the Indian Ocean created a unique demand for the WLED systems. Many of the lights had already been installed in some of the mountain villages of Sri Lanka when the tsunami hit the island nation. Refugee camps that sprung up after the disaster also needed lights, and Sarvodaya, the largest and most established NGO (non-governmental organization) in Sri Lanka, asked Dave for one thousand lighting systems, and it was expected the request was to exceed ten thousand lighting systems over the following year. Each system cost $50 US, and Dave set out to raise the staggering amount.

It seemed impossible. Dave confided in an old Scottish soccer buddy in Ottawa who had his own company and who, without any warning, sent Dave a tiny card in a tiny envelope during the summer of 2004 containing a cheque for $200,000. He still remembers the moment he opened the envelope: "I'm in tears, I don't know what to say."

Six months later another tiny card arrived with another cheque—this time for $25,000 for what was now dubbed the Tsunami Refugee Camp Lighting Project.

In another part of the world undergoing massive rebuilding— post-Taliban Afghanistan—the LUTW project was approached in the fall of 2005 about providing lighting systems for villages.

Meanwhile, honours continue to come in for Dave and his colleagues. In May 2005, Dave received the Meritorious Service Medal from Governor General Adrienne Clarkson. The citation read:

"Since its inception in 2000, the project has provided low-cost lighting to more than four thousand homes in dozens of remote villages around the world. Through this inspirational undertaking, Professor Irvine-Halliday has enhanced the health and safety of many communities, fostered local education, developed an economic infrastructure and protected the environment."

Dave Irvine-Halliday's life changed dramatically after that eye-opening hiking trip in 1997. From engineering professor to fundraiser, he has no regrets.

"This is the single most important thing I'll do in my life," he says.

The sixty-two-year-old professor is amazed that he is even around to do it. He nearly died three times in his life. His first brush with mortality happened as a teenager when he was in a motorcycle accident—a drunk driver hit him and Dave's head was slammed into the curb. Years later, he survived an avalanche while climbing in Europe. And he lived through a horrific fall while climbing Ben Nevis in Scotland. Somehow, he managed to climb off the mountain with a broken leg.

"God was keeping me for some reason," he says.

Maybe he was spared for a purpose. Maybe that purpose was to be the spark that ignited the Light Up the World movement. In any case, he can't think of anything he'd rather be doing.

"I'm living my dream."

From left, Janine Journault, Youlia Smykova, and Jessica Journault on their tire swing in 1995. Alberta families found room in their hearts for the kids of Chernobyl. (Photo by T. J. Georgi)

Children of Chernobyl

Into the arms of strangers

On a summer day in July 1995, *ten families stood outside the legion hall in the town of St. Paul, Alberta, waiting anxiously for a bus to arrive. These families were about to host a group of out-of-town kids for the summer, but these were no ordinary kids.*

These kids came from the other side of the world. They didn't speak English, and they would have to be watched very carefully during the two months of their visit for any health problems that might arise. That's because these little strangers grew up under the spectre of a radiation cloud ten times worse than what was created by the atomic bombs dropped on Nagasaki and Hiroshima at the end of the Second World War.

They were the Children of Chernobyl.

The children arriving in St. Paul came from the Bykhov District, Mogilev Region of the Republic of Belarus, which was part of the Soviet Union that fateful day back in 1986 when the Chernobyl nuclear power plant in neighbouring Ukraine experienced a melt-down. Mogilev was one of the areas most affected by the disaster. By

1995, the Soviet Union had split up, and Belarus and Ukraine were now independent countries, but both nations still had to deal with the ramifications of the Chernobyl incident nearly a decade earlier.

The families waiting for the visitors to arrive were nervous and not sure what to expect.

Janine Labrecque, one of the host moms, recalled later: "I didn't know what people expected—that they'd be alien kids or something."

Caroline Bailey, another host parent, said her church supported her family's decision to host a child even though "I had a lot of fears and reservations at first."

Added Janine's husband, Guy: "We thought it would be a good experience for our kids. That was one of the main things."

Janine knew instinctively that this was going to be a good experience. She had always wanted to travel the world, and hosting a child from Belarus, she thought, would be like bringing a little bit of the world right into her home.

Vicki and Eugene Journault home-schooled their four kids on their farm outside St. Paul. Vicki was always looking for ways to enhance their learning, and then she heard about the Children of Chernobyl. "It was exciting, meeting a little person from a country we've never visited," she said.

Finally, the bus pulled in. It must have been an overwhelming experience for the ten children from Belarus, many of whom had already travelled for twenty-two hours straight before landing in Montreal and spending the night there in the care of a church group. This was all before beginning a further cross-country trip to east-central Alberta via plane to Edmonton and then a bus trip (sponsored by CFRN-TV of Edmonton) to St. Paul. The parents and host kids had to be patient. There would be time enough to get to know their visitors—time enough to learn what they had experienced in their short lifetimes.

Valentina Lopatko, a representative of the Belarussian Charitable Fund for the Children of Chernobyl, who accompanied the kids as translator and chaperone/surrogate mom, knew exactly what they'd been through. She remembered 26 April 1986 as a sweet spring day in the city of Minsk, at that time the capital city of the Byelorussian SSR. Her husband was away visiting his mother, and Valentina, who taught English at the university, was getting ready for her first class of the day.

Miles away, the unthinkable had happened in a nuclear power plant in the neighbouring Soviet republic of the Ukraine, something that would have far-reaching consequences for Eastern Europe and for the whole world. It was a group of scientists in distant Sweden who first stared at their data in disbelief and then sounded the alarm. A major nuclear power plant in the USSR, surrounded by cities and towns, was hemorrhaging radiation. The worst nuclear disaster in history had occurred and its name would haunt us forever: Chernobyl.

"The people who went to save the power station didn't know the consequences. They had families," Valentina recalled. "I wasn't very scared. At the time I didn't know what consequences would arise."

The city of Chernobyl, located twenty kilometres south of the power plant, was evacuated. People were told to take nothing with them. In an effort to prevent looting, valuables like furs and jewelry were taken to the cemeteries to be destroyed. Before long, symptoms of radiation sickness started to appear in the population. People became pale and were sick all the time. They had problems with their lungs and boils erupted on their skin. Others lost their hair.

Once the danger filtered down to people living in the regions bordering Chernobyl, panic reigned. They knew they were in trouble but what, exactly, were they supposed to do about it?

"They washed the pavement, took away topsoil in places," Valentina remembered. "First, they tried to import food."

Fresh produce was contaminated, and nothing grown in the area was safe to eat anymore. Cattle were slaughtered and their carcasses buried. There was a macabre joke floating around—or was it a joke?—that someone wrapped a cow in cellophane to protect it from the radiation, only to let it eat contaminated grass.

Like something out of a science fiction movie, the radiation made plants grow to enormous size. "Everything is extra large," Valentina said. Children couldn't resist eating the contaminated mushrooms, currants, and other wild fruits. It was too late for precautions but many didn't know it. "Moms were told to shut their doors and windows and don't let the kids play outside."

In the months that followed, people died of cancer in record numbers. Valentina knew of one boy who lived with an elderly grandparent because both of his parents had died. The orphanages were overflowing. Families were given an extra month's allowance to cover the cost of an extra loaf of bread—or for coffin money.

It's estimated that between six hundred thousand and nine hundred thousand children were in the path of the radiation, and Belarus received approximately seventy per cent of that contamination.

In the years following the disaster, well-meaning experts thought children exposed to this horrific atmosphere would have a better chance at living healthy lives if they could leave their contaminated homeland for six to eight weeks a year. Twenty-three countries, including Canada, and three hundred and fifty organizations rose to the challenge and offered to sponsor therapeutic visits away from the Belarus–Chernobyl region.

Parents had to make difficult decisions: keep their kids close by during a difficult time, or send them halfway around the world into the arms of strangers, if only for a few months. Many of the children involved in the program were only babies when Chernobyl melted down; they had never known life without radiation.

In faraway St. Paul, Alberta, Sandra Greer heard about the opportunity to host the children. "I think we first heard about the program in March 1995," Sandra recalls. "My husband, Murray, first heard about the Chernobyl program on the radio. Murray and I wanted to help and do our part in making a positive difference in the world. We believe in '. . . inasmuch as you did it to one of the least of these my brethren, you did it to me,' [from] Matthew 25:40."

Sandra approached Albert Blazey, coordinator of the St. Paul Learner Centre, with the idea. With the trip only a few months away, the organizers had only a month to raise the $17,000 needed to cover the costs. In the nick of time, one organization after another came forward to sponsor a child.

But hosting a group of ten children involved more than just providing a roof and a bed. The kids would need trips to the optometrist and the dentist. They'd need haircuts. They would need supplies to take back with them to Belarus. The community wanted to make sure the children would want for nothing during their stay.

When the Children of Chernobyl got off the bus in St. Paul they were greeted by everyone from town dignitaries to Member of Parliament Deborah Grey.

After the fanfare died down, the kids got to meet their host families. Janine and Guy Labrecque met nine-year-old Yourie Protassov. Paul and Caroline Bailey collected Alexandre Narovski, a ten-year-old who went by the nickname Sasha. Vicki and Eugene Journault finally got to meet their visitor, nine-year-old Youlia Smykova, while Sandra and Murray Greer took in a little girl named Marina Chitikova.

The travellers had only to make one final, short journey—the few kilometres from the legion hall to their temporary homes around the St. Paul area, in Bonnyville, Two Hills, Elk Point, St.Vincent, and nearby acreages. Once there, the host families were faced with the challenge of making their visitors feel comfortable.

The kids from Belarus had brought with them small packages of gifts and family photos to give to their Canadian hosts. Paul Bailey remembers sitting on the floor and playing Lego with Sasha, when suddenly the little boy got up and went to his room, coming back with gifts for everyone, such as a pen for Paul's daughter, Rachel, with Russian lettering on it. She was thrilled.

Across town, Yourie had a little notepad with his hosts' names written down and brought out gifts for each member of the Labrecque family. After he gave out the toys and puzzles, he ran off in shyness, but he was very proud to be able to give the gifts, host mom Janine said afterward.

The children's parents in Belarus had also written letters for the Canadian hosts. These were ordinary working people: a teacher, a cook, a museum worker, a night watchman, city workers, and farmers. All were worried about how their kids would manage on their own in a foreign country.

"He's afraid of the darkness," wrote one worried mom. "He needs a light on." Another mom advised that her son was allergic to orange juice.

Yourie's mom pleaded: "He's afraid of the water. Please don't make him go swimming."

Youlia's mother, a school cook in their small village, wrote that it was a great honour for her daughter, as Youlia would be the only one from their village to make the trip.

"I'm crying as I write," she wrote, adding that, while the Chernobyl disaster happened near their home, it was a disaster that affected the whole world. But, she wrote, this trip would connect two families who would otherwise never meet. "That's a good thing that came out of a bad thing."

Youlia told her host family how her father, a locomotive engineer, tried to prepare her for a visit to a continent he'd never even seen himself.

"If you go to the church, behave," he warned, as Youlia had only been to a church once before in her life. "If you find something strange in the family, don't laugh," was another piece of advice. Youlia's father had also given her a crash course in perfect table manners.

Valentina stayed with each family for a few days, acting as a translator and troubleshooter, but most of the time the hosts were left to accommodate children who couldn't speak English. It was one of the things the families had worried about, but soon they noticed something wonderful happening. The host kids and their visitors quickly developed their *own* language, part English and part Russian. They were communicating.

Before long, the visiting kids had started to pick up English. Yourie, for example, learned a few English phrases such as, "Pass the juice, please." The first time he said this, in perfect English, his hosts nearly spilled the juice in surprise.

In the Journault household, Youlia fit in quickly, playing with Vickie and Eugene's daughters, nine-year-old Jessica and eleven-year-old Janine. After her first week, Youlia was even heard to ask, "Where is Dad?" when Eugene, a heavy equipment operator, was called out of town on business.

One day things became quiet at the Journault house—too quiet for a household full of children—two boys, two girls, and one visitor. Vicki searched for the kids, only to find them all downstairs performing a play using a shower curtain for a theatre curtain. At centre stage was Youlia, her hands in a pair of slippers and her sweater on backwards, acting out a character.

"The children came up with that without having a mutual language," Vicki said in awe.

In another host house, Yourie's bright smile and thoughtful ways appealed to Janine Labrecque. He always helped out when it came time to prepare meals, and they didn't have to mow their lawn once while Yourie was there.

The families saw their visitors blending in to their family routines. At Vicki and Eugene Journault's acreage, Youlia insisted that she not be a burden to the family.

"Right away, she [Youlia] wanted to help with the chickens," Vicki said. Youlia said she had a little dog, Bim, and ten rabbits at home, so she was used to this type of work, helping out in the garden and around the acreage when she wasn't playing with Penny the dog or bouncing on the family's trampoline.

Like Yourie, Youlia insisted on repaying her host family's hospitality by doing her fair share (and sometimes more than her fair share) of household chores. It wasn't unusual to find her simultaneously helping Vicki make lunch and folding clothes from the dryer. Every morning, she would check on the family's two rabbits as soon as she woke up.

"She doesn't know that I know, but I've seen her," Vicki said at the time.

When the host families spoke about their guests, one could be forgiven for thinking they were speaking about their own children. The distinction between stranger and family became blurred almost from the first day.

Vicki liked to talk about how Youlia learned the fine art of making water balloons. But she always put *warm* water in the balloons before they met their target, Vicki said quickly. This was one considerate kid.

Janine Labrecque found Yourie "a real teaser. He likes to win you over. The house lit up when he smiled."

Added Guy: "He has a kind of presence. He's mostly a cheery guy. He'll kind of carry the moment if things are tense or rushed."

Yourie couldn't get enough ice cream, a treat almost unheard of in Belarus because of its expense. The same was true for Sasha, but he had to learn the art of eating ice cream. At first he tried to bite off the top of the scoop; the shock of the cold on his teeth was a lesson he no doubt remembered. After that, he let his ice cream melt and it dripped all over. By the time he was half-through his cone, all the other kids had finished theirs.

Youlia didn't like green beans, but she loved pizza the first time she ever tasted it. She also loved to sleep in, cuddling in under her cozy covers for as long as she could.

Most of the Children of Chernobyl were only nine and ten years old at the time of their visit to St. Paul, so the inevitable bouts of homesickness soon set in. The kids knew how far they were from home, but for many of them, it was impossible to contact their loved ones back in Belarus.

This made for a bittersweet summer for Youlia Smykova, who celebrated her tenth birthday half a world away from home. She missed her mom, dad, and two brothers more than she could explain to her host family. Sometimes a faraway look came into her eyes, and they knew she was thinking about her family thousands of miles away. But the Smykovas had to rely on a distant neighbour for the phone, and such calls were reserved for emergencies; Youlia was on her own.

"For my children to know that she hasn't had contact with her mother . . . she's very brave to do that," Vicki said, adding she hung a calendar beside Youlia's bed, marking the days left before Youlia got to see her mother again.

One day the Labrecques took out some maps of Eastern Europe, hoping it would encourage Yourie to talk about his home. To their surprise, it had the opposite effect.

"He went to his room and closed the door," Janine said. She followed him. His eyes were misting up and he pushed her away. Later, she noticed that whenever he seemed down, he made himself really busy.

Sasha was also homesick at first. Caroline noticed that her own son, Justin, took on a role she'd never seen him play before.

"Justin was a little mother to him," she said. "If he would cry, he'd go over and hug him or he'd bring out a game. Justin was the one who would comfort him."

Not-so-random acts of kindness were commonplace during the kids' visit. When Sasha lost his wristwatch at the pool, someone bought him a waterproof one. Another time, two of Guy's co-workers took Yourie on a shopping spree to buy clothes.

It wasn't only adults getting into the act. Janine Journault, Vicki's oldest child (age eleven at the time), shyly confessed that she'd bought a hair band for Youlia's birthday with her own money. She pleaded with her mom to keep it a secret from Youlia so it would be a surprise.

Numerous supplies like snow boots, snowsuits, and cough syrup were provided for the children to take back home.

"Our child, Marina, her family didn't even own a hand can opener," says Sandra Greer. "We all sent the kids back with a lot of stuff and some money. All the children were given free dental and optical work and supplies as well, thanks to very generous donors in St. Paul."

In fact, there were so many offers of clothing and supplies that the kids couldn't possibly have taken it all back with them. But then again, this was St. Paul, the place where Mother Teresa chose to send her Sisters of Charity. Giving is a community tradition.

The Children of Chernobyl weren't confined to St. Paul during their stay. Youlia experienced her first genuine Alberta rodeo and got her picture taken with the cowboys. She wanted to know why the horses bucked and Eugene Journault did his best to explain. Kids from Belarus also went on camping trips, saw the Rockies, attended the Camp Kiev Vacation Bible School, and paid a visit to massive West Edmonton Mall, where they enjoyed the rides of Galaxyland.

On one outing, Yourie—whom his mom described as being afraid of water—conquered his greatest fear. "We took him to the lake and you couldn't get him out of the water," Guy said, laughing.

The children had arrived in Canada with their own preconceived notions about what it would be like. Yourie knew it was a large country across the ocean and that it was hot, while others thought it would be a cold place, like Siberia. What did they think of it after living here for awhile?

"Beautiful," Yourie said. "It's a very good country. I shall tell my fellow students about Canada," he said through Valentina's translation.

Said Sasha: "There are a lot of cars here. The shops are very large."

Caroline and Paul Bailey loved Sasha's amazement with everything. Everything was exciting to Sasha and he soon learned the words "wow" and "cool." It gave the couple pause to reconsider what they took for granted.

"We're so prone to complaints sometimes, but we get an idea of what we do have through their eyes," Paul said. Added Caroline: "Seeing our lifestyle in such a different view, we began to appreciate what we have."

Janine Labrecque agreed. "He's taught us what's important in life," she said. "It's not the *things*. You don't need all the things."

The success of the original reason for the visit—to improve the kids' health—is hard to measure. It's not certain what long-term medical benefits, if any, this trip provided, beyond an undeniable boost to the kids' morale. Only time would tell. Most of the kids gained weight during their stay in Alberta and the dark circles disappeared from under their eyes. There were no signs of the headaches, nosebleeds, and fainting spells that they suffered back home.

Towards the end of the summer, Youlia, who had arrived with chest congestion and sunken cheeks, was looking much better. "She's such an outside girl. That's helped a lot," host mom Vicki said.

There were some minor concerns. One child found a strange lump while in St. Paul but a doctor couldn't find anything wrong. It was probably just a part of natural development, Valentina said, but these children were more familiar with cancer than with normal development.

The original plan was to take every child out of the Chernobyl–Belarus region for six to eight weeks each year for maximum health benefits. That was optimistic, Valentina said. Despite the experts' high hopes of sending each child away from Chernobyl once a year, most of these kids would never get another chance. Money was the major obstacle.

"We must help ourselves," Valentina said. "We must find a way out. We do our best to help the children survive. They are our future."

Vicki tried to teach her own kids about Chernobyl in the days before Youlia arrived. Nuclear accidents and radiation can be a tough lesson to teach, let alone learn. Having Youlia live with them was the best lesson they could ever have, she said.

"It left us wanting to know more," Vicki said wistfully, adding that her daughter hoped to someday travel to Belarus and visit Youlia.

Maybe the most important thing about the trip was for the kids to know that people cared. Yourie was asked what he would tell his family when he arrived back home.

"I will tell them that I've got a lot of friends here. I felt very well here," he said.

Sasha said the Baileys were very kind, and Yourie liked the Labrecques very much. What would Yourie tell his own family about them? "The husband is rather tall and very kind. The lady is very large-hearted," he said.

Guy later joked that Yourie said he looked like Russian premier Boris Yeltsin.

Youlia thought that the Journaults were very kind to take her into their home as their "fifth child." But Vicki was modest about her family's contribution to this project.

"It's not difficult. If anything, it brings more life into the family. It's a gift," she said.

The Journaults would not soon forget their summer with Youlia. In spite of her homesickness and health problems, the little girl touched them with her spirit. Asked what they would remember after she returned to Belarus, Vicki replied, "Her smile. She's always smiling."

Early on the morning of 10 September 1995, a small group of families again waited for the bus in St. Paul, but this time the bus was going to take the Children of Chernobyl on the first leg of their long journey back home to Belarus.

Valentina tied a label on each small suitcase, "Children of Chernobyl," a reminder that these kids had to go back—to loving families, to be sure, but also to a life lived amongst radiation and an uncertain future. But the kids were happy and excited—they were going home! They were too young to realize that they would likely never see these kind strangers again.

The bus arrived and started to fill. A sob or two could be heard in the crowd and a couple of the Canadian kids needed a hug as they watched their friends leave. The kids of Chernobyl waved goodbye from behind tinted windows. And on the other side of the world their parents waited for them.

Ten years later, life has slowly returned to many of the regions laid waste by the Chernobyl disaster. Many of those whose lives were shattered by the meltdown of 1986 have worked hard to rebuild what once was lost.

By 2006, the Children of Chernobyl were young adults, perhaps attending university, or working, or perhaps starting to raise families of their own. Or, perhaps, the visit to Canada came too late. We may never know.

Most of the visitors were unable to keep in contact with their host families after returning to Belarus, and to this day families such as the Journaults, the Baileys, and the Labrecques—the everyday heroes of St. Paul who opened their hearts to these kids—hope to someday learn what became of their young visitors.

Even though the families lost touch, perhaps the experience can best be summed up in the words of the late Albert Blazey: "They'll know that on the other side of the world, people have a heart."

Nicki, an English Springer Spaniel rescued and nourished by the Senior Canine Rescue Society, at home in her new back yard in 2002.
(Photo courtesy Megan Brown, Nicki's adopted "mom")

Jude Fine

For the love of fido

It all began in 1993 with a fluffball of a miniature toy poodle named Meagan.

The thirteen-year-old weighed only two and a half pounds, her emaciated body about half the size it should have been. She was running loose in Calgary, obviously lost and more than a little scared, when her rescuer brought the abandoned dog into the Calgary Humane Society for adoption and into Jude Fine's life.

A part-time employee and dedicated volunteer with the organization, Jude was immediately taken with the small orphan.

"She was bubbling over with joy," Jude recalls. "She had so much joy and so much zest for life despite the fact she was so neglected."

Since most people planning to adopt a pet are looking for a younger animal, Jude knew Meagan's prospects of finding a new home were minimal at best. If someone didn't adopt her within a reasonable period of time, the society would have had no choice but to euthanize her. Jude decided not to take that chance and adopted the dog herself.

"I didn't know if I would have her for three weeks, for three months, or for three years when I adopted her," Jude says, but she took the chance, made a home filled with lots of love and attention for Meagan, and before too long the small orphan started to put on a little weight and her health improved.

"It turned out I had her for three years before she died," Jude says, adding she learned first-hand how wonderful senior dogs can be as companions. "Just because they're old doesn't mean they [can't be] valuable family members."

The experience got Jude thinking that it isn't fair how so many older dogs find themselves homeless. Sometimes it's because their owners have died or moved into a nursing home where pets aren't allowed. Sometimes senior dogs require more veterinary care than their owners are able to afford. Other unfortunate dogs suffer plain and simple neglect. As a result, many loving pets find themselves abandoned at the end of their lives, through no fault of their own.

Jude began scanning the Internet, looking for senior dog rescue groups to see if there were ways she could get involved in this type of work. It wasn't long before she realized there really weren't any groups focusing on senior dogs in Canada at that time, and the only organization in the United States was the Senior Dogs Project out of San Francisco, founded by Teri Goodman.

"I called her and since then, we've become great friends," Jude says. The two women encouraged each other in their common mission. Teri launched a website for her project in March 1997; Jude wasn't far behind, and by September of the same year, the Senior Canine Rescue Society (SCRS) of Calgary had a website of its own and was in full swing.

News spreads through the Internet like no other medium, and before long Jude's efforts were being recognized across North America. Two online discussion groups were set up, opening up the topic of senior dog adoption to anyone interested in the issue worldwide. Ironically, for the first while, the Calgary-based organization was better known internationally than at home, Jude recalls.

Names of senior dogs in need of homes and veterinary care started pouring in. There were Katie and Beauty, Abbey and Maggie Mae, Nakita and Kiya, and so many others.

"When I first started, senior dogs didn't have a prayer in a shelter," Jude says. But through her efforts and those of her American counterpart, the word spread that senior dogs can be quality family pets. More and more people opened their homes, adding their voices to the relatively small number who sounded the alarm that dogs were dying needlessly, simply because no one would adopt them.

The SCRS began as a volunteer-run, non-profit organization that relied heavily on donations of dog food and money, and on the kindness of foster families who were not only willing to open their homes to orphaned dogs that were waiting for permanent homes, but were also willing to pay the veterinary bills for those animals that were ill.

The society could only handle so much, however, so Jude had to set up criteria for the dogs she would accept.

"Our specific focus is to accept dogs from owners who have passed away, have gone into nursing homes, or are ill and unable to care for their senior dog any longer," Jude says. Only rarely does the society take in owner-surrenders.

"We don't take in a huge number of dogs," Jude says, explaining the personal investment is considerable, and there just aren't that many people able or willing to make that kind of commitment. Once a dog is in foster care, she says, it could be there for quite some time before an adoptive family is found.

"We've had dogs in foster care for a year before they've found a home," she says.

Although the society usually has no more than twelve dogs in foster care at any one time, Jude finds it hard to say no when she hears of a dog in need. As a result, she often finds herself taking in a dog or two more than she had planned, especially when a senior dog in poor health is discovered.

"If we take in a dog in poor health, we don't adopt it out . . . they just stay as a foster dog," Jude says, adding that the goal in those cases is to make sure the dog has the best quality of life possible in its remaining days.

Jude established criteria for choosing foster families. Prospective foster families have to understand their role is as short-term caregivers and that the dogs in their care may be quite ill and need extra attention. During its time in a foster home, the dog is observed for any behaviour or health problems that need to be reported to a prospective adopting family. That way, if it is determined that a dog isn't good with children or other animals, or displays potentially challenging behaviour, the adoptive family is well informed before they make their decision.

Aside from possible health issues, foster families also have to understand that when they take in a senior dog they're taking in a dog with a sometimes-turbulent personal history. That dog may have lived a wonderful and happy life with a single owner until a situation arose and that caregiver had to relinquish their valued pet, or the owner passed away. These aren't just situations where Fido doesn't get his Kibbles 'n Bits. These are situations that can leave an animal in a state of pain and grief.

"In one situation, an owner had passed away and his dogs had been with the dead body for a few days before it was discovered," Jude says. How does an animal cope when its human caregiver isn't responding to the usual good morning wake-up call? In a situation like this, a pet needs extra care and understanding. It's for this reason that Jude and the members of her organization do not place new arrivals into adoptive homes until they have been in foster care for at least a month. That way any behavioural idiosyncrasies can be discovered and made known to families interested in adoption.

"We promise our adopters no surprises and I'm very, very proud of that," Jude says.

Since quality of life is the major issue with every adoption, there are times when putting a dog down isn't something even Jude can argue against. "You have to do what's in the best interest of the dog," she says.

Each dog is special, but every now and then a dog shows up that blows even the most ardent dog-lover out of the water. Nicki was just such a dog. The purebred English Springer spaniel was discovered abandoned in Montana in 2001. Emaciated and half-bald from mange, the seven-to-eight-year-old dog wouldn't have survived much longer without some kind of human intervention. That's when Jude and the SCRS went into action.

"We have over seven hundred volunteers who help move rescue dogs," Jude says, explaining that the only document needed to ship a rescued dog over the border from the United States to Canada is a record of its vaccinations. "We've had dogs from Idaho, Washington . . . if we can get drivers we can work everything out."

Nicki made her way to Canada just fine, but she was in sad shape.

"It was the most challenging rehabilitation case we've ever had,"

Jude says. "It was five months before we were able to put Nicki up for adoption."

There was no shortage of families willing to open their homes to Nicki. People from across the country learned about the dog through the SCRS's website and began e-mailing Jude, asking for updates on her progress and expressing their interest in adopting her.

For Jude, it was easy to see why so many people were interested in adopting Nicki. The dog was regal and held her head high, despite her physical condition—a true survivor.

But Jude was concerned; she didn't want a family to adopt Nicki out of pity. In her eyes, Nicki was far too proud an animal for that. It took some time, and a considerable amount of discernment, before the perfect family appeared.

"I read an e-mail from a family in Saskatoon," Jude says, explaining that the lengthy message touched her in a way that was indescribable. "Even though we found her in such a terrible state, she never lost her dignity, and wherever she was adopted I wanted her to be a queen." The family adopted Nicki and she lived with them for another four years, despite her health problems.

"Her owner carried her around all night," Jude says, thrilled that Nicki was treated like a queen to her dying day. And even after Nicki passed away, her adoptive family remained involved in senior dog rescue. "There's a whole legacy from this dog who stole so many hearts."

Foster and adoptive families don't necessarily require acres of land, even if they plan to adopt a larger senior dog. Instead, what they really need is loads of love, some large, soft pillows or a cozy dog bed, and patience. More often than not the rescued dogs give back much more love than they receive.

Over the years, the SCRS has placed about five hundred dogs in safe, loving homes.

"That's a really small number when you compare it to some groups," Jude says, remaining humble in her accomplishments. Still, there's no arguing the fact that her involvement with Teri Goodman and the subsequent Internet publicity spurred other concerned individuals to organize similar dog rescue groups—something Jude is incredibly excited about. Jude sees good communication as one key reason for the success of the SCRS, so she makes sure its website is filled with information, including profiles of the dogs available for adoption, complete with their likes and dislikes.

Jude herself also continues to adopt dogs when she has room and was taking care of six orphans during the summer of 2005. She doesn't see herself as any kind of hero. Instead, she remains grateful for the efforts of every volunteer, for every donation.

"We're very grateful to people who open their homes and hearts to senior dogs," she says. "We're just a very small piece of the puzzle."

Barb Tarbox visiting Louis St. Laurent Junior/Senior High School in Edmonton. Her final days were devoted to disseminating a single message: stop smoking.
(Photo courtesy Tammy Beakhouse and John Contessa)

Barb Tarbox

Just one life

Who can forget the stark image of the tall, painfully thin woman standing on stage in her faux leopard hat? Who can forget her in-your-face panache when she whipped off her hat to expose a bald, emaciated head?

Barb Tarbox could be controversial, even shocking, but she had an important message to convey and very little time to get it out to young people who, like herself, had started smoking long before they could even drive a car. Now, what was once thought to be just another bad habit was going to make her pay the ultimate price.

If she could reach just one life, before hers was taken . . .

Barb had no thoughts of being a celebrity or a hero on that August day in 2002 when her doctor found something abnormal on her X-ray. A CAT scan revealed tumours on her heart, lung, and bronchial tube—it was cancer. By September, they discovered the cancer had moved to her brain. Her remaining life could now be measured in months, not years. She was only forty-one years old.

It was with a feeling of enormous guilt that Barb had to tell her child, nine-year-old Mackenzie, and her husband, Patrick, that they were going to lose her, all because of her addiction to cigarettes.

Fighting the cancer was one of the toughest challenges yet for a woman who'd had more pain in her life than most people could imagine. Her mom had died of lung cancer when Barb was twenty-two. In 1990 Barb gave birth to twins who were born prematurely and who lived painfully short lives. One twin, Patrick, died after only two weeks when an infection spread through the hospital ward; her other twin, Michael, died at the age of eight of a heart attack caused by an undiagnosed congenital heart defect. And now, Barb Tarbox faced death herself.

She wasn't going to let cancer take another life, not if she could help it. Somehow, a message had to be delivered to the young people of Alberta. That's why Barb set out on a gruelling speaking tour when she was in the final stages of her cancer, at a time when others might have chosen to spend their remaining days in the comfort of home.

Barb thought if she could get just one kid to quit smoking, then it would all be worthwhile. For that, she would do anything—even use up her last days on Earth.

The first time many Albertans heard the name Barb Tarbox was in September 2002 when she participated in a Kids for Cancer Run at Edmonton's Malcolm Tweedle School. After that baby step, it was time for her to tell her story.

She started with a tentative speech on 29 October 2002 at T. D. Baker Junior High in Edmonton, where her niece, Ashley, attended school. Her audience that first day consisted of only thirty students. Barb wasn't a trained speaker; she had to learn the art of public speaking on the fly, at the same time she was also learning first-hand about the horrors of cancer and chemotherapy. Steadily, as her confidence grew, she found herself able to share more details with the young people she spoke to.

Just one life . . .

Illness and death used to be discussed much more frankly in our society. We've come a long way from the days when dead relatives were routinely laid out in their caskets in the family parlour. Today, death is almost a taboo subject in our world. One of the biggest events in our lives is the end of it, and yet we cloak it in dark mystery. Cancer is treated the same way. Obituaries tell of a person dying "after a courageous battle with cancer." It's neat and clean and it masks the vile truth. We especially try to keep these harsh details of life from our young people.

Not Barb.

"When you receive radiation to your brain, oh, boy—_this_ is what happens," Barb told the kids at one school, tearing her hat off her head, revealing her bald, pale scalp. The young faces around her looked like they'd been shot. "Yes, it is gross. *Yes,* it's uncomfortable. *Yes,* I hate it and this is what smoking got me. Look at it!"

Barb did not spare them her tears, her anguish, or her love. These kids—some as young as Grade four—who could spot a phony better than many adults, were listening as though their lives depended on it, and as far as Barb was concerned, their lives *did* depend on hearing what she had to say.

Barb couldn't bear the thought of her little girl without a mom, and she shared her anguish with the kids she spoke to, many of whom had not even experienced their first kisses yet.

"What happens when somebody hurts her feelings; or she gets her first crush on someone; and she graduates? I'm not going to see any of it," she said through her tears. "I don't want anyone walking this road. I'm dying because I smoked. I can't bear the idea of saying goodbye to my family. I just want to hold them forever."

The first school administrators to hear her talk must have been in shock. But the unruly kids who had been herded into the gym just minutes before were now silent. Teachers and principals stood there in amazement.

Barb broke all the rules. Not only was she talking about cancer and death—her own—she admitted that it was her own fault. She had made a fatal mistake when she was just a kid.

In Grade seven, Barb, who was born in Edmonton to Irish immigrant parents, moved from a small school to a large one. She wanted to be popular. On the surface, she had it all. She was six feet tall and an aspiring model with phenomenal clothes.

"But I wasn't with the popular kids," she said later.

These kids had parties and always hung out together. To Barb, they looked like they were having so much fun and she desperately wanted to be a part of it.

"But they were all smokers. So, I started smoking," she said. By the time she finished Grade nine, Barb was smoking a pack a day, but in Grade nine you feel like your whole life is still ahead of you. Barb was a star athlete—track team, basketball, volleyball, downhill skiing, water sports—but by Grade ten she no longer had the stamina to try out for even one team. Barb never made the connection, and she kept smoking.

And those popular kids who smoked? Barb didn't even see them again after Grade nine.

Barb hid the cigarettes from her family at first, but eventually they found out about her habit. Her mom disapproved, but she was a heavy smoker herself. What could she do? And Barb seemed to have the world at her feet. After high school, she launched a modelling career that took her to the catwalks of Ireland and England. But in 1982, she returned to Canada to discover her mother paying the ultimate price for her own smoking habit. Barb would later share these painful memories with students.

"Nineteen years ago, my mother was diagnosed with terminal lung cancer—long-time smoker. And her doctor—Dr. Tommy Fields—said to me, 'Barb, do you smoke?' He said, 'If you don't quit smoking, I'm going to see you here in twenty years.'

"I thought, 'No, no, no, I'm going to quit—but later. I'm going to quit.' Well, nineteen years later, I have terminal lung cancer."

It was an ugly, ugly topic to share with kids whose world likely consisted of little more than homework, sports, and video games. Barb didn't spare her audiences the gruesome details. She forced them to face the truth.

"The greatest obstacle I have grows within me. It grows every second, every minute, every hour, every day—and it doesn't stop. Nothing can stop it," she said.

She brought along her radiation mask and passed it around so the students could see it and touch it. It was made of stiff white mesh, molded to the exact shape of Barb's face. It looked like something out of a science fiction movie, but it was painfully real. She told them that during treatment you can't move your cheeks, and you can't move your chin; you can't even blink.

"This [the mask] is locked into place on the table," Barb said. "You cannot move. Think about it. And when you're lying there you get direct voltage of rays—radiation. Know what it does? *It burns your skin.*"

And, of course, she lost her hair—a common side effect of radiation treatments.

"Forty-one years of hair gone in ten days—just like that," she said. "After forty-one years of hair, you get rather attached to it."

She spoke about her tumours. One was massive, attached to the lower temporal lobe in her brain. But the scariest one was also the scariest to the students who sat looking up at her.

"It's growing right beside the aorta of my heart and any second it could grow over my aorta. Instantaneous death," she said. "This is where smoking gets you, guys."

The tumours affected her strength and motor skills. Once accustomed to navigating the catwalk, Barb could sometimes barely get herself from place to place.

"I was walking down a hallway and I dropped. I dropped." She told them she sat on the floor, willing herself to get up. "Nothing works. Nothing works."

Barb told them about shopping for groceries one time, the day after Halloween. Such were the effects of the treatment on her appearance, she had to wear heavy stage makeup when she went out, as well as a hat, even indoors. A little boy about five years of age was sitting in a shopping cart when Barb passed by.

"Mommy, someone should tell her Halloween's over," Barb recalled the youngster saying. It must have been a blow to the heart for a woman who once was a model.

Despite all this, Barb could not quit smoking. The doctors told Barb that it would do no good for her to quit now—her cancer was too far advanced. She probably couldn't have quit, anyway. Some people insist it's harder to quit cigarettes than it is to kick a heroin addiction. Unfortunately, Barb was criticized for still smoking while talking to young people about quitting. She hated being seen buying cigarettes as she became well known for her anti-smoking campaign; a friend offered to buy them for her.

For Barb, it was more proof of how deadly this habit was. Even faced with terminal cancer, she couldn't quit. And she shared this with the students, too.

"I smoked. I never tried to quit. Found every excuse, guys," she said. "I don't want any one of you feeling this. I don't want you feeling this pain. You don't deserve it. You know better than this. You are so above it. I wish I had quit smoking. I wish I had never started. But I started. I didn't quit.

"I am dying—a hundred per cent of smoking."

Barb Tarbox, more than anyone, proved that smoking is not just about the smoker. She told how smoking had devastated her family. The ones who didn't smoke seemed to be hurt the most. Smoking is often considered a personal bad habit, but one tolerated by society. We look the other way. It's the person's own choice, after all, and we think it's no worse than drinking alcohol. But this attitude is changing, and even smokers themselves are beginning to acknowledge it.

Barb quickly found allies in her mission. Heather Crowe, an Ontario woman also diagnosed with lung cancer, was in many ways the polar opposite of Barb. While Barb had been a smoker for decades, Heather had never smoked a day in her life, but she worked for forty years in a restaurant where the air was blue with smoke every day; her cancer was believed to be the result of second-hand smoke. She and Barb briefly did some anti-smoking campaigning together, trying to get smoking banned in public places. One woman had made the choice to smoke, the other hadn't, but they were facing the same fate. Crowe, who was in her fifties, was the first person in Canada to successfully claim for full compensation for lung cancer caused by occupational exposure to cigarette smoke. During her first round of chemotherapy in 2002, she wrote to all of the federal, provincial, and territorial ministers of labour and requested the laws be changed to protect workers from second-hand smoke. Crowe, whose cancer went into remission for several years, would ultimately outlive Barb Tarbox and continue to fight her cancer into 2006.

Within a few months of starting her campaign, Barb was a familiar sight on TV screens across Alberta and beyond. Broadcasters ran Tarbox's stark, plain-spoken public service announcements (PSAs) regularly. There were no flowery messages, no advertising agency-inspired images, just Barb in front of the camera, her bald head revealed for all to see, speaking from her heart. The spots were hard to watch, but that was the point. Barb Tarbox forced viewers to forget about *Law & Order* for a few minutes and face reality. The media, hardened souls who report death on a daily basis, were moved to tears by her presentations wherever she went—around Alberta and Toronto, to Ottawa to meet the prime minister and members of the House of Commons, and on to Vancouver, Victoria, and Montreal. Thousands of e-mails were rushing in from people all over the country.

Within a few short months, she'd gone from the local Edmonton news to CBC's *The National*. She even caught the attention of the *Montel Williams Show* in New York, which gave her a chance to start spreading her message to at least a small segment of the American public.

Barb was getting better and better at reaching her target audience with every new appearance.

She was also growing sicker by the day.

<hr />

Barb Skowronski, then a Grade twelve student at Louis St. Laurent Junior/Senior High School in Edmonton, was one of the many who saw Barb's messages on television. Several years later, she still remembers the impact of those PSAs and how they inspired her to help spread Barb's message.

"I couldn't believe the things that she was telling people," Barb S. says. "I wanted her to come and talk to the students at my school."

At that time, about a quarter of Barb Skowronski's friends smoked. She used to hang out with them outside, just off the school grounds where smoking was not forbidden. They were her friends, but she hated the fact that they smoked.

"I would tell them that it's bad for them and that they could die. I'd even show them pictures of people with cancer," she says. It didn't have much of an impact, but when she saw Barb Tarbox on TV, the younger Barb knew she'd found the answer.

She and her friend Ashley Bourget sent an e-mail to Donna Gingera, who had volunteered to handle Barb Tarbox's public relations. The girls asked how Barb was doing and if there was any way she could talk to the students at Louis St. Laurent sometime in the spring of 2003.

The reply was a setback. No, Barb wasn't doing too well, Gingera wrote, and it was unlikely she could continue her talks to the schools.

The girls were disappointed, but they understood. A few weeks later they got another e-mail: Yes, Barb Tarbox *would* be able to do it after all. Gingera advised them to talk to their principal to make arrangements.

"We quickly went to his office and told him all about it," Barb S. recalls. "You could tell that right then he was really happy that [we] as students would organize something like that without having someone tell us to."

Principal Brent Patterson was touched by the girls' initiative.

"At first he said that it was just going to be for the senior high students, but then me and Ash told him that a lot of the younger kids should know because lots of them were already smoking," says Barb S. "That was when he decided to have it for the whole school."

It was a good plan. Barb Tarbox had started smoking at age eleven.

Barb S. and Ashley set up posters around the school to let students know Barb Tarbox was going to talk to them. It was a tough sell at first.

"Lots of the students didn't really care that she was coming," says Skowronski. "Lots of the smokers didn't even want to listen to her. The way they thought of it was, 'How is this lady going to tell me to stop smoking when she's *still* smoking herself?'"

But many other students were excited to have Tarbox come to the school. They'd seen her on TV and heard so much about her. She had become something of a celebrity. It got kids interested in listening to her message.

The talk was scheduled for 17 April 2003. Not only Louis St. Laurent students, but many from neighbouring Harry Ainlay Composite High School were there; the gym was packed.

Barb Skowronski and the school administration waited anxiously. Barb Tarbox had already survived well past the few months it was estimated she would live with her type of cancer. At any moment they expected the phone to ring with the message that she was too sick to do the talk—or worse, that she had passed away.

By this time, Barb Tarbox was sleeping for much of the day, and was now using a wheelchair on a regular basis. Her doctor told her that she was too unsteady on her feet to use a cane, and her friends tried to convince her not to make any more public appearances.

It was amazing that she was even alive on 17 April, let alone well enough to fulfill her commitment to speak at just one more school. But she had a job to do.

Just one life . . .

"The first time I saw Barb she was getting pushed in her wheelchair by her husband and they went into the staff room of our school," Barb S. recalls. She and Ashley, as the organizers of the event, were allowed to go in as well. "We got to have a nice little chat with her. We talked about all sorts of things, not just the fact that she was dying of cancer. We just talked about life in general. I remember how when I went to hug her, I could just feel how fragile she was."

And yet, that day Barb Tarbox got out of the wheelchair and walked into the gym at Louis St. Laurent, supported by her cane. The gym was bursting at the seams with more than twelve hundred kids waiting to see what this woman, who was dying of cancer but still couldn't quit smoking and who could take a turn for the worse at any moment, would tell them.

The waiting wheelchair, the projected images of Barb and her family, the empty intravenous bags she held up, all told the students and staff of Louis St. Laurent that this was a woman with a final message. She told the students flat out they had to stop smoking and convince their friends to stop smoking.

"You could save their life. That's not exaggerating. *You could save their life!*"

Principal Brent Patterson, hovering by with the wheelchair in case Barb collapsed, had never seen his students so affected by anything. He saw big Grade twelve boys crying, and others who were barely holding back the tears until they could leave the gym. The younger students—the ones he wasn't sure should hear her at all—were deeply affected. There was absolute silence. The kids listened. They listened.

"Honestly, if a pin were to drop, we would hear it," Barb S. recalls. "She yelled. She wanted to get the point across. She was angry at herself and wanted everyone to see that.

"The one thing I will never forget is when Barb was talking about her daughter and how she had to tell her that she was dying. And no one knows how long she will live as Barb was telling us about all this."

As she finished her talk, the students, especially the younger ones, rushed in to meet her.

"They couldn't get close enough to her," recalls Brent Patterson.

They were crowding her and the adults realized she was having trouble getting air. The wheelchair was quickly put to use but Barb continued to talk, touch, and hug.

The kids had listened. Even when they wouldn't listen to one of their own peers talk about the dangers of smoking and show them pictures of people with cancer, they were drawn to Barb Tarbox. She'd exposed those two taboos—death and cancer—in a single swoop.

Did it work? Patterson says it is hard to say definitively how many kids quit smoking as a result of the presentation, but they found fewer cigarette butts around the school and fewer kids were seen going outside to light up for some time afterwards.

"I think that Barb was clearly the only one that actually made a final decision for them," Barb S. says. "Some of them even quit after hearing her talk. But sadly, some still smoked. I think that the ones that *did* smoke finally realized that it's not 'cool' after all, that there are lots of bad things that come along with it."

Many Louis St. Laurent students paid tribute to Barb Tarbox on the Internet.

One student named Jenna posted this message on the website of the Alberta Alcohol and Drug Abuse Commission (AADAC): "Whenever I want a cigarette, I always just think back to when I was hugging you and when you were speaking to the school. I received pictures of us together and I carry them around with me all the time."

Kirsten, another Louis St. Laurent student, wrote, "I have NEVER seen our whole school be so respectful in the last three years that I have gone there . . . It was dead silence except for the occasional stifled sob from those crying . . . I will NEVER smoke again . . . even if everyone else smokes, she can know that she saved just one life . . . just one."

Just one life . . .

In the 2003 Louis St. Laurent yearbook, there are pictures of Barb Tarbox taken during her visit. In one she looks dwarfed by the hundreds of students who came to hear her speak. In another, there's a close-up of her hugging a tearful student.

The talk at Louis St. Laurent turned out to be Barb Tarbox's final public appearance. Her health continued to deteriorate and when she died just one month later, on 18 May 2003 at the age of forty-two, her death received national press coverage. In the less than seven months since she first started spreading her message to kids, she had managed to reach fifty thousand students across Canada, and who knew how many more with her TV news spots, talk-show appearances, and AADAC PSAs?

"Her passion was with the young people," Patterson says with reverence in his voice. "She became such a figure in Canada for the young people."

Barb Skowronski says meeting Barb Tarbox had a profound impact on her life.

"I only met Barb that once, but that did it for me," she says. "Everything that she said impacted the way I thought of things. As the days went on, and the more I thought about it, it started changing my life. I finally started realizing that more than just one person suffers and there really isn't anything good coming out of smoking."

Why did Barb Tarbox touch so many kids when anti-smoking campaigns costing millions of dollars often didn't work? Students told her that they'd seen all the Health Canada warning labels on cigarette packs. One of the Health Canada warning labels has a photo of a diseased lung, while another shows the damage smoking can do to a person's teeth. But Barb knew it wasn't enough to reach their minds—you had to reach their hearts.

The AADAC website received hundreds of e-mails in the days just before and after Barb Tarbox's death.

"I was recently on my way home from work on the bus, and I was reading the paper when I came across the article on Barb Tarbox. By the time the bus had come to my stop, I made my decision to quit right then and there as it touched me deeply," wrote Tim.

"I am taking your advice to help people who suffer from this addictive drug. My stepmom has been a smoker for 24 years and now with my help she is finally quitting. If it wasn't for you and your profound presentation I probably wouldn't have taken the action I am now," wrote Logan.

"[Barb] touched people throughout the world. I smoked for 20+ years, I will be 38 in a few weeks and I quit March 1, 2003. I can't think of a cigarette now without thinking of Barb," wrote Lenore in Minneapolis. Someone named Nick reported from London, England, how he had heard of Barb Tarbox and her work during a visit to Northern Ireland.

At least one message on the AADAC site provided proof that Barb's mission to stop at least one kid from smoking at the age she started had been a success.

"I'm 14 and I'm in Grade 9. My first time smoking was in Grade 6 and I've stopped. She's got through [to] me and I hope she got through [to] a lot of others," wrote Maureen.

And one message was left by Crystal, a woman whose own life seemed to in some ways mirror Barb's: "I am a 29-year-old mom of two little girls age two and six . . . you said if you could reach just one person . . . Well, you did! My husband and I both went on the patch Monday the 13th and you were the inspiration for it . . . I am very grateful to you for sharing your precious time talking to the public, and to your husband and daughter for sharing you with us! I watched my step-grandparents die of cancer, my Dad has emphysema, but none of that did it for me. But you, Barb, you made something go Click in my head."

Just one life . . .

"I know I should have thrown the cigarettes out. I didn't. And now I'm dying at forty-one. I've planned my own funeral. Let me tell you. I've picked my own music for the funeral. I've devastated my husband of twenty years and my daughter. You can't get this kind of pain. It's just not worth the cigarettes. You have to quit smoking." –Barb Tarbox in the video, *A Life Cut Short by Tobacco*.

"Promise me you'll quit smoking, or you'll never start, or you'll help others. I want you to have a phenomenal life. I'm gonna miss you." –Barb Tarbox in the video, *Memorial*.

They wouldn't take no for an answer. Alberta's calendar girls are, from left, Janet Hutsulak, Yvonne Adair, and Audrey Shillabeer.
(Photo by T. J. Georgi)

Alberta's Calendar Boys

Not on our watch

The death of any library is a tragedy, yet that's the fate the Lakedell
Public Library near Pigeon Lake, Alberta—the smallest public library in
Canada—faced in 2002. Supporters of the library, which served ten
summer villages around Pigeon Lake, two counties, and the Pigeon Lake
Reserve northwest of Red Deer, needed to raise at least $300,000 to buy
a new building or the library would close.

When the Lakedell Public Library was established in 1968 at
Lakedell Elementary School, it was the last public library in Alberta
to be set up inside a school building. The rationale was to have the
school library and the public library under one roof for the conven-
ience of students, and at the same time allow adults who came in to
use the public library to serve as positive role models for the kids.

"There was a little boy who said he couldn't wait to grow up
because then he'd never have to read another book," says Lakedell
Area Community Library Society (LACLS) member Janet Hutsulak.
"It just seemed right to have him see adults coming in and enjoying
books."

Yvonne Adair joined the staff of Lakedell Elementary in 1972.
Over the years, Yvonne changed roles within the school—starting as
a teacher's aide, then as school librarian and secretary, and eventually becoming librarian of the public library.

"Nobody ever asked me if I'd do the public [library]—it was just
there and I did it," says Yvonne, laughing.

Yvonne soon discovered that her latest job involved more than just filing books. She had to fight to keep the public library going. One time she even approached the school board and said, "I want the same [funds] that you get for basketball, which you're losing all the time."

In 2000, the Lakedell Public Library was down to a 3.0- by 4.5-metre space in a corner of a classroom. As the school needed more space, the public library section became smaller. It had become virtually impossible for the library to provide many of the services expected of a public library, such as interlibrary loans. Pam Mitchell, who took over as librarian when Yvonne retired in 1999, had no space to pack books.

"She'd have stuff on the floor and she'd be packing on a little kid's table and it just got really ridiculous," says society member Audrey Shillabeer. "We were supposed to have three thousand square feet. We had one hundred and fifty. We couldn't buy books because there was no room to put them."

The library had to cram six thousand books into its tiny space. "The best way to know if our book stock was up or down was if there was an inch of bookshelf open or not," says Audrey, adding the library serves as many as four thousand permanent residents year-round and as many as twenty-five thousand cottagers and vacationers during the summer.

The library also faced a challenge by 2000 that could not have been predicted in 1968. Security had become of prime importance in schools, and administration now had to know who was roaming the halls at any time. As a result, access to the public library became restricted; this went against the philosophy of a public library, where everyone is welcome, no questions asked.

"People were feeling uncomfortable coming into a school during school hours," says Janet.

It was time to either close the public library or move it to a different location.

The County of Wetaskiwin, the municipality that governed the library, was asked if it could help the LACLS find a new location. Incredibly, the society was asked to provide a forty-year business plan.

"They just want it to look like a business, and it's not going to ever look like a business," Audrey says. "I think that just like any government they've got finite resources that they have to give to roads, buildings—all of that stuff, and the library has been a very small part. They said there will be no more money for libraries."

The society had to start thinking out of the box if its library was going to survive. With spunk and determination, Yvonne told the council, "We are the little old ladies who are not going away."

Yvonne had a great idea for a fundraiser. She could hardly wait to bring it to the next meeting of the LACLS.

"Are you right out of your mind?" the members demanded. "Pose nude? For a calendar?"

Yvonne had hoped for a better response. After all, it had been done before, and very successfully.

Yvonne had recently seen the movie *Calendar Girls*, the true story about a group of middle-aged women in the small North Yorkshire town of Knapely, England. They wanted to raise money to buy a leather couch for the relatives' room of a local hospital, in memory of a beloved husband who'd recently died. The women shocked their national Women's Institute and the entire country when they decided to pose nude—or nearly nude—for a calendar to raise the money.

The English women reached their goal and bought the leather couch. In fact, they raised enough money to build a new wing of the hospital. Their story became an overnight sensation in Britain and for a time they were darlings of the world's media.

Despite this success story, the members of the LACLS flatly refused to try the same thing in Alberta. Their clothes would stay on, thank you very much.

"I said—no, no, we'll get the guys. The guys!" Yvonne told them. "I'll get my son and my grandson, and Vicki will get her husband and her son and . . . " Yvonne continued naming the male relatives of the women staring back at her with open mouths.

It took three meetings before the members could be convinced. Audrey Shillabeer had seen the movie, too, and was one of Yvonne's first supporters. Two other members of the society, Vicki Duggan and Janet Hutsulak, also joined in. Putting out a nude calendar was a drastic step, but maybe drastic was just what was needed to keep the Lakedell Public Library afloat.

The society finally gave in to Yvonne's enthusiasm and agreed to give the calendar idea a try. The first person Yvonne approached to pose for the calendar was her forty-three-year-old son, Ken.

"Mother, I can't do this," he told her. "Naked? Are you nuts?"

By now Yvonne was used to having her mental capacity questioned on the subject.

"Ken, keep your bathing suit trunks on," she said. "You *have* to do it. You and Dallan [Ken's eighteen-year-old son] are doing it."

Audrey's husband, son, and new son-in-law agreed to pose—"They were volun*told*," she said. But Janet's husband, Verne, was aghast at the idea.

"I don't even like looking at *myself* with nothing on," he protested. Good cause or not, he refused to strip.

The women started looking beyond their families; after all, they had twelve months to fill. One by one, recruits were lined up, including a local farmer, a retiree who lived in a cottage on Pigeon Lake, a real estate agent, and a chef. The twelve months were coming together nicely.

Audrey wanted someone special for the December page. She asked friends, "Who in this area has a character face and would look really good in the calendar?" Three people suggested John Evans, the owner of Hilltop House, a restaurant at Mulhurst Bay on the lake. John looked like he had stepped out of a Norman Rockwell painting; they had found their Santa.

Now that they had the models lined up, they needed a photographer. Audrey thought of an old high school classmate, Ron Layzell, who was now a photographer with his own studio in nearby Wetaskiwin.

"I phoned him up and said, 'Here's a voice from your past,'" Yvonne recalls. She asked him if he'd seen the movie *Calendar Girls*. He said no. She quickly explained it and described the project they wanted to do as a library fundraiser. Would he be interested in photographing nudes, and what would he charge?

"He immediately said, 'I will do it for the cost of film, and I'll check out the movie.'"

The photo shoot was set for 10 August 2004. Leon Strembitsky of

Caelin Artworks of Wetaskiwin agreed to be the project's art director. Most of the photos would be shot at Layzell Studios in Wetaskiwin, except for Ken Adair's photos, which would be shot at his home.

"Leon worked alongside Ron to produce our beautiful photographs in spite of the raucous assembly masquerading as logistics and staging in the next room," Audrey recalls.

As befitting a calendar dedicated to a library, each photo showed the model reading.

Darrel Fipke, whose wife is a partner in a local spa called Essentials, was shot reading while sitting cross-legged on a massage table. He would be Mr. January and also appear on the calendar's front cover.

Earl Marney, the retiree from the beach, was immersed in a wine book for February. On the bottom of his page was his quote, "The beach, fine wine, and good books: retirement is everything it's cracked up to be!"

Mr. March was Luke Jevne, Audrey's son. A firefighter, Luke was tired during his photo shoot, which came at the end of a long shift. Luke's hobby is diving so he was photographed with snorkelling equipment while reading about his next diving holiday.

"As an avid scuba diver, he was embarrassed because the flippers he's wearing aren't diving flippers—he has snorkelling flippers on," Audrey recalled. Luke was worried that a real diver would notice the difference; he was more worried about that than he was about posing nude.

Mr. April was Jim Duggan, the real estate agent, who brought his briefcase along. Ron had him sit on it. Audrey heard Jim say, "Gonna have to boil this now," as he left after the shoot. When the photos came out, Jim would take considerable ribbing because of a "Reduced" sign seen lying at his feet. Later he would leave a message for Ron: "I know I waived all rights to this, but I want you to tell me if any of them laugh at me."

Dallan, Mr. May, was the youngest model at eighteen years of age. He had his picture taken reading a book behind his Yamaha YZ125 bike.

Audrey's husband, Ian—Mr. June—is a golfer, so he was shot posing with a set of golf clubs. Yvonne teased Ian that he was able to "hide" because he wore a kilt in the photo.

"He looks like he's wearing a full kilt but he isn't," Audrey explained. Ian wore a length of tartan cloth draped over his shoulder, down to the knee. He also had a golf bag. Audrey went in with him and arranged the props and clothes, then left before Ron took the pictures.

The society was fortunate to get Jay Toole, one of Audrey's neighbours, to pose for July.

"He is shy. We're lucky he did it," Yvonne says.

Jay was a bit of a local celebrity as he was scheduled to work on the Brad Pitt movie, *The Assassination of Jesse James*, which was to be filmed in the Calgary and Edmonton areas during the summer of 2005. He was going to supply some horses and drive a wagon in some of the scenes, so Ron photographed Jay reading behind a saddle.

Mr. August, Tim Wood, the chef at the Eco Café at the Village at Pigeon Lake, sat on a table that Audrey used as a desk. A pot full of fresh vegetables was strategically placed in front of him—too strategically, as it turned out, as one corn cob ended up in exactly the wrong—or the right—spot in the photo.

"He's had corn jokes ever since," Janet says.

"And that was *not* set up that way," Audrey insists.

It was important to the organizers of the calendar fundraiser that people realized nothing sexual was intended by any of the photographs.

"It was simply a money-maker and a laugh," Yvonne explains. "Just a lark."

Audrey added that the idea was "to get a message out about reading, and positive images of men. So the corn happens to be there— and that *is* an honest mistake."

Honest mistake or not, the photo had the potential to be controversial, and the organizers were particularly worried about what Tim's wife, Debora, would think.

"Well, God made him and He made the corn, too," she replied to their great relief.

Back at the photo shoot, Audrey's son-in-law, Trevor White, who owns a restaurant in Drayton Valley with her daughter, posed as Mr. September.

"We wanted to show that he was a proud Native," Audrey says of Trevor, who is of Cree and Métis descent. Ron photographed him sitting on a blanket and working at his laptop computer.

Gary Schmidt, Mr. October, is a local farmer and a great spokesperson for the whole community. He was glad to bare all for a good cause.

"He came in that day and it was fine haying weather," Audrey remembers. It was the supreme sacrifice for a farmer to give up a perfect harvest day, but it showed his commitment.

Merrick, Vicki's son, was Mr. November. A hockey player, he was photographed on a bench with his hockey equipment around him.

"He came in just like he was a movie star," Audrey says. "It was so funny. He was just so nonchalant."

At last came Mr. December, John Evans.

John made for a perfect Santa, sitting at an antique desk and looking as though he's checking his list to see who has been naughty or nice. Yvonne compared the shot to a classic Norman Rockwell painting.

One more photo was taken for the back of the calendar, and the honour went to Ken Adair, Yvonne's reluctant son, who agreed to do it if he could pose with his car, a 1957 Chev Bel-Air.

The project was completed and, thanks to Ron's artistic skills, the society had created a calendar to rival that of the original Calendar Girls.

The society then had to choose a day for the unveiling. Vicki suggested 1 April 2005. Not only did April Fools' Day seem apropos, it would give people plenty of time to buy it for Christmas gifts, since the calendar was for 2006. The project was kept a closely guarded secret until then.

"We kept this under wraps," Audrey says, pun intended. "I didn't want exposure at that time."

Adds Yvonne: "We didn't want anybody to steal our idea."

The 2006 *Lakedell Public Library's FUNdraising Calendar* was ready to go. To promote the calendar, Audrey came up with the idea of quashing the myth that men don't read by using short sentences that were reminiscent of an old school primer; Vicki added her editing skills and the theme became: "Look. Men read. See men read."

The calendar features each model's thoughts on reading. On the back are quotes from then Alberta Lieutenant-Governor Dr. Lois Hole (who passed away several months before the calendar was released), Ian E. Wilson, the Librarian and Archivist of Canada, and Premier Ralph Klein. The two men were also asked to pose for the calendar.

"It's the most difficult thing to write," Audrey says. "How do you say, 'By the way, would you like to pose naked for us?'"

"We asked Klein and he declined," says Yvonne. "We actually asked Klein to sit behind his desk with just a tie."

One wonders if he read the request personally. But whatever the premier's personal thoughts on the subject, back came a polite form letter with, "Best wishes for success in your fundraising efforts."

Ian Wilson's response was more lively: "Encouraging people to 'strip' away their inhibitions and discover what can be found between the covers is essential to the success of your project."

On 1 April 2005, the calendar launch ceremony was held at the Village Creek Country Inn at the village at Pigeon Lake.

"We were thinking maybe fifty [would attend]," Audrey says.

The society couldn't have guessed the reaction their calendar would have. Instead of the predicted fifty people, there were two hundred eagerly awaiting the unveiling. Then came the interviews—CBC TV and radio, CFRN TV, Global TV, Literacy Canada, the *Edmonton Sun*, and local papers—to name just a few. The producers of the CBC documentary series *On the Road Again* also expressed interest in the project.

After the CBC aired a feature about the calendar on its *Canada Now* national newscast, Audrey got a call from an old friend in Montague, PEI.

"Well, well, well!" he said. "What happens when I'm looking at the news and there's Audrey and her band of naked men? Better send me one or two [calendars]."

Yvonne had a similar experience. A friend from Prince George, BC, told her: "I never watch the news from Edmonton. But guess what I saw on TV today? What are you up to now?"

The focus on the novelty of the calendar did not surprise the society members.

"The media was really focused on the guys being naked rather than the guys reading," Audrey says. "They really, really glommed on to the nakedness, which of course we knew. It is the story.

"I wished once in a while they would say, 'What is the problem behind this? Why are you fundraising?' It was glossed over and they would interview the models and say, 'What's your life about?'"

Orders for the calendars came in from as far away as Alert in Nunavut, Australia, and England. The initial goal was to sell 2,500 calendars and raise $50,000. About $8,000 of that would go to production and other costs, leaving $42,000 to be put towards the new library fund.

"It sure beats bake sales," Audrey said.

By anyone's estimation, the calendar was a success, but not everyone was happy about the project. Yvonne's brother, for one, was a little upset at the idea, considering it pornographic.

"We didn't come into the world with cowboy boots on," Yvonne pointed out.

One woman accused, "You've even got a kid in there," referring to Dallan.

"I said, 'No, that kid is mine and he's past eighteen,'" Yvonne shot back.

Two letters came forward to protest the calendar. One was sent to the society and the other was mailed to a local paper, but because it wasn't signed, it wasn't printed.

In a startling parallel to a similar scene in the *Calendar Girls* movie, one person even told Janet that she didn't see why they couldn't have used nice pictures of Pigeon Lake instead.

Another woman, whose family had just returned from Rome, told Yvonne that she, too, disapproved. Yvonne said in that case she hoped they didn't visit the Sistine Chapel and take a good look at the paintings.

"You know, when you're negative, that's okay because we get people a little more interested in it," Yvonne told her. After that, the woman never said another word about the calendar.

"One of the ministers of a local church condemned it from his pulpit," Janet says. "There were maybe one or two people in his congregation who didn't buy it because of it, but far more came to see what the fuss was about."

Even Yvonne's brother eventually came around.

"You shouldn't really be condemning it until you've seen it," Yvonne told him. He responded, "I don't want the calendar but here's twenty bucks."

Even one of the women who protested the calendar ended up

donating five hundred dollars to the cause. Janet, likewise, found herself receiving twenty-dollar donations from people who weren't interested in the calendar, but wanted to support the library.

Yvonne's daughter-in-law, Cheryl—Ken's wife and Dallan's mom—was thrilled with the calendar.

"She ran to the high school where she used to work and she just had a new grandchild but she was promoting the calendar before her grandkid's picture," Yvonne says, adding that Cheryl and Ken bought twenty-five copies.

Not surprisingly, women are the best customers for the calendar, including many older women. Yvonne took it to a girlfriend's seventy-fifth birthday party, along with a cookbook.

"You can have one of these for your birthday. Not both," Yvonne told her.

"I'll take the cookbook," her friend replied. Yvonne tried to hide her disappointment. "And I'll buy the calendar," her friend finished. "In fact, I'll buy two calendars."

One librarian in Wildwood had five calendars mailed to her under secret cover, as she planned to give them to co-workers as gifts.

Men, on the other hand, don't know what to do with the calendar.

"They want to have it in their hand and then they kind of just give it away, right away, like they shouldn't have it in their hands," said Audrey.

As the money came streaming in from calendar sales, other more traditional events were held to help boost the library fund even more, including strawberry teas, a Mother's Day brunch, a generous donation from the Pigeon Lake Lions' Club (more on this later), and even a slightly dangerous and often dirty venture:

"One fundraiser [involved] Yvonne's bottles," Janet explains. "She picked bottles and had people bring bottles and cans to her house all summer. She's raised about one thousand dollars."

By September 2005, there were only six hundred calendars left to sell, and they were prepared to commission another print run of five hundred calendars as the end of 2005 approached.

By all accounts, the fundraising drive was a huge success. When they totalled their fundraising and other efforts, added in a Community Facility Enhancement Program grant from the Alberta government, and included money banked over the years from the library's book-buying budget (since the library had long run out of space to add new books), they now had well over half the money needed to buy a building.

It was a phenomenal feat—and the patient was now off life support.

By the fall of 2005, the society was more than halfway to finding the money they needed for a new building on their own. There was no need for a forty-year business plan, no waiting for municipal funding that wasn't coming, and something incredibly positive was happening. The bold move to produce the nude calendar had attracted lots of attention. It also renewed interest in the library within their own community, which, except for a few doubters, seemed to be very proud of the accomplishment.

In September 2004, the society finally had to move the Lakedell Public Library out of the school that had been its home since 1968. "The school did not ask us to move," says Audrey. "We found the location untenable: space, access, signage . . . and other issues."

Just when it seemed the library would be homeless, two people came forward and donated a ninety-three-square-metre mobile home for them to use, rent-free, until the new building could be purchased. Once the Lakedell Library settled in its new, albeit temporary home, the number of visitors immediately tripled.

Around this time, Lori Fipke and Cheryl Semeniuk, owners of the local spa, Essentials, approached the society with another fundraising idea.

"Cheryl and I were talking and we'd like to do a gala night for you as a fundraiser. We'll do it all and just give you a cheque at the end," Lori suggested.

It was a huge success. The calendar guys appeared in tuxedos to sign calendars. They had a gala dinner, a "fun casino" with a murder mystery, and a silent auction to top it off. The group sold a thousand dollars' worth of calendars alone, and the night brought the effort seven thousand dollars closer to its goal. As of early November 2005, some $210,000 had been put on the fundraising board.

"We've just been rollin' along," says Yvonne.

After such a successful year, it wasn't long before the society members started fielding questions about what they would do next. Was there another calendar in the works?

"The buzz in the community now is: It's the women next! It's the women next!" Audrey says.

A reporter from Edmonton's CFRN TV asked Yvonne if she would consider becoming a member of Alberta's own Calendar Girls.

"I said, I guess if everybody else stepped up to the plate I'd have to, meaning the rest of the [society], but knowing full well they wouldn't," Yvonne says, laughing.

Still, ideas were already swirling about the sequel. One idea, which would have to be photographed after the library found its permanent new home, would feature pictures of people using the library—at the computer, standing behind a stack of books, checking books out—all in their birthday suits, and all tastefully done as before. Then again, blank cards with the pictures of the calendar boys would look spiffy, too.

The society also shared ideas with other small libraries about fundraising. The Movement for Canadian Literacy in Ottawa approached them about speaking at their international convention in 2006, and the society realized that public speaking might be yet another source of income. Who wouldn't want to hear how a small public library survived in part by creating a nude calendar, and more importantly, why the organizers felt they had to do something so beyond the norm?

The future now looks bright for the Lakedell library. On 7 November 2005, the county council approved the society's plan to purchase its own building. On 10 January 2006, the society bought a ten-year-old commercial building in Ma-Me-O Beach, with a possession date of

1 March. The new location put them closer to the people they serve—the children who access summer programming at the beach, a store-front school that has no library of its own, a small First Nations community of avid readers, and researchers and job hunters.

"A perfect spot all round, and we could not be happier," Audrey says.

The fundraising continues.

Yvonne and her colleagues have two words of advice for other small libraries looking for ways to survive: "Go big."

"Go passionate about your mission," Yvonne says, a living example of her words.

Adds Audrey: "Definitely this group has a culture of 'yes.' You've got to say, 'Yeah! We can do it!'"

Sometimes you just have to have the courage to ask for the moon. During its fundraising drive for Lakedell Public Library, the society approached the Pigeon Lake Lions' Club asking for the outrageous sum of seventy thousand dollars. To their pleasant surprise, not only did they receive half of their request, they were told that more might come the next year, "just because we went in and asked them," Yvonne says.

"We're not exceptional in any way," says Audrey. "We're representative of people in most small communities. Every community has these people that step up to the plate."

If you live in the city, you might take it for granted that you have a good public library. But when you see a library in a small community, chances are it's there because someone fought for it, someone who passionately believes in knowledge and learning. At every chance to vote it down, downsize it, or build an overpass instead, someone was there to say, "Not on my watch."

"I say Yvonne is the keeper of the Lakedell Public Library," says Audrey. "She's the one that is passionate and committed. How many people will go through garbage for bottles to fundraise for it?" Or, for that matter, convince a dozen men to bare all for the cause?

"Some days I reflect back to our days, not so very long ago, of being so crowded when we were sharing that classroom, and man! We sure had guts! To decide to move, to invest in a calendar, to not give up," Audrey says.

"I would never have given up," says Yvonne. "This is my heart and soul."

Jeff Liberty with his dog, Nova. The Olympic diver plunged into the icy waters of the Bow River to rescue a woman in her car.
(Photo courtesy Calgary Fire Department)

Jeff Liberty

Olympic hero

Jeff Liberty once stood in the footsteps of giants, competing for the glory of Olympic gold on behalf of Canada at the 2000 Sydney Games. Although he didn't make it to the podium, he was still happy to have placed nineteenth out of fifty athletes in the diving competition.

A little over a year later, his skills and athleticism would be put to the test for a much more valuable prize—the life of a woman and her unborn child.

The cool, crisp November 2001 morning when Jeff Liberty started out for his daily walk through Calgary's Southland Park with his fiancée, Nicole Podoleski, their dog, and another couple didn't seem particularly out of the ordinary. It was a typical late-fall day, and although there was no snow on the ground, the chill in the air made the advent of winter unmistakable. Southland Park is a natural, ungroomed park and a popular off-leash area for dogs that is nestled between the Bow River and the bustling Deerfoot Trail freeway.

It's been said life happens when you least expect it, and the saying proved especially true on this day.

"We were just walking along, a normal day, and all of a sudden we hear a crash," Jeff recalls. "We looked to the left, towards the Deerfoot Trail, and saw a car had veered off the Deerfoot and was coming through the off-leash area.

"It was just like the scene out of the *Dukes of Hazzard* when the car takes off over the bridge, but this one didn't make it."

The foursome watched as the car careened through the park, launched off a 1.5-metre embankment, and landed squarely in the waters of the Bow River, about five metres from shore. By the time the bystanders reached the banks of the river, the trunk end of the car was beginning to sink, and its driver, twenty-two-year-old Shannon Roberts, appeared to be in shock, grasping the steering wheel and staring straight ahead.

Recognizing that the driver didn't appear to be moving, and not knowing if the person was unconscious or worse, Jeff stripped down to his boxers, jumped down the embankment, and leapt into the icy waters. The experienced diver had little fear of the river though this was far from the controlled conditions of the diving tank.

"I swam up to the car and knocked on the window," Jeff says. Shannon finally responded, looking over to Jeff as he motioned for her to roll down the window. Although she managed to roll it down slightly, once she heard and felt the water seeping into the car she froze, grabbing the steering wheel with both hands once again. But the window was open just wide enough for Jeff to get his arm inside.

A coincidence made the rescue a little easier for him.

"The car was a little Chevy Cavalier, and at the time we [also] had a Cavalier, so instinctively I knew where the handle was to roll down the window," Jeff explains.

"I reached my arm in the window. I tried opening the door first, from the outside and inside, but it wouldn't open. It was locked. So I reached in and rolled down the window the rest of the way. Then I reached in to her, undid her seat belt, and managed to pull her out the window."

Just in case Jeff did have any problems, his friend Russ Gavan was standing by on the shore, also stripped to his boxers and holding a large rock in his hand, ready to break the windshield if Jeff couldn't get the window or door open. Russ, a water polo player, was no stranger to the water, either.

"He [Russ] was on the shore and he helped bring her up," Jeff says. By this time, the paramedics and the fire department had started to arrive—but they might have arrived too late for Shannon Roberts if Jeff and his friends hadn't been in the right place at the right time.

"By the time I got her out of the car and to the edge of the water, the car was completely under," Jeff says. "The only thing you could see was a bit of the antenna."

Jeff's dog, a two-year-old black Labrador named Nova, had been apprehensive the entire time Jeff was in the water and was anxious to see her master.

"She was trying to get to me in the water, so my fiancée had to hold her. And then, when I was at the edge of the water, she [Nova] came down beside me," says Jeff.

While the dog's main concern might have been to reconnect with her master, Jeff's main concern was a more practical one.

"I went and grabbed my clothes and put them on—I was freezing," Jeff laughs.

Once dressed, he went to check on Shannon to make sure she was okay. "By that time, EMS was there and they had everything under control; they put her in the back of the ambulance and went on their way," Jeff says.

Jeff and his fiancée went home, still feeling a little dazed about what had just happened. The first thing Jeff did was try to warm himself up in the bathtub.

"I don't know how long I was in the river—probably only about five minutes—but it felt like forever," Jeff says. "After everything was over, the fire rescue took the temperature of the water and said it was around 36°F [2.2°C]. It was pretty cold."

In the short time it took for Jeff to make it back to his apartment, his adventure had already made the news on most local radio stations, and his telephone wouldn't stop ringing.

"My dad was calling, my mom was calling," Jeff stops for a moment, as if he is still confused as to why the incident captured so much attention. "I think it was because it was just after 9/11 and people were looking for something positive to think about.

"It was really surreal. I didn't want any attention for it. I guess it's just the way I am—if I can help, I will help. I just figured, if it were the other way around, someone would do the same for me. I didn't really think I'd get any recognition from anyone."

The irony of the situation seemed to have escaped him at the time, despite its being repeatedly pointed out to him how a potentially tragic accident ended happily because Jeff, an Olympic diver, just happened to be in the vicinity at precisely the right time. In fact, he downplayed his chosen specialty, pointing out he wasn't that great a swimmer and the only benefit his diving experience had on the situation was that he was comfortable in the water.

"I've been diving ever since I was eight—I grew up in a pool, basically," he says. "I started diving before I really knew how to swim. And then I learned how to swim and when I'm around water I'm comfortable . . . it doesn't scare me at all."

To think the situation could end in anything other than a positive outcome never crossed his mind.

"In the back of my head I knew everything would turn out fine— you know, that I could get her out," Jeff says.

But the story had one final twist. It wasn't until Jeff Liberty was reading the media reports about the accident that he learned that Shannon Roberts was not only a diabetic, but she was also three months pregnant. The importance of his life-saving effort instantly doubled.

_____

In the days following the accident, Jeff returned to the park to reassess the accident site for himself.

"I checked out the fence where she came through and then I followed her tracks," he says. "There was a big orange pole in the ground—it's fairly deep in the ground—and if she would have hit that it could have been a lot worse. I stood right beside the pole and where her tire tracks were and I couldn't fit in-between, so she missed it by inches. And if she was more to the right, she would have hit a big cluster of trees, so I'm glad she did go where she went, into the water."

The cause of the bizarre accident was not immediately known. It was thought, at the time, that either a tire had blown or that Shannon had experienced a diabetic reaction of some kind. When Jeff spoke with her later, her memory of the incident was sketchy. Fortunately, she was only in hospital for a few hours and was unharmed.

"I remember talking to her and she said when she woke up she wasn't feeling well, but she just thought it was from being pregnant. She was on her way to get groceries," Jeff says. "She remembers driving down Deerfoot Trail and the next thing she remembers is me tapping on the window telling her to roll down the window . . . so she doesn't remember going through the park or anything."

It was later determined that Shannon had indeed experienced a diabetic seizure.

Jeff never worried about his safety throughout the ordeal, nor did Nicole.

"She knew I wouldn't put myself in harm's way," Jeff says, brushing off the thought he was in any real danger.

The timing of the accident was fortunate—it could have been much worse. The park is popular with dog lovers, but because it was a Monday there weren't a lot of people out that day—a miracle in and of itself, as far as Jeff is concerned.

"It wasn't a weekend day so everyone was back at work, thank God, because normally that park is packed with people and dogs," he says.

Jeff is grateful he hadn't started out either five minutes earlier or later for his daily stroll. He is also grateful that he was familiar with Shannon's model of car, making it that much easier to roll down the window and find and unclasp the seat belt. And the fact that Shannon was in shock, rather than in a panic, and didn't fight any of Jeff's rescue efforts, actually eased the situation.

Captain John Conley, Public Information Officer for the Calgary Fire Department, told the *Calgary Sun* after the rescue that Shannon was fortunate Jeff Liberty was nearby when the accident happened.

"It could have been a different story if someone like him wasn't around," Conley said.

Despite the fact that Jeff didn't think his actions warranted any recognition, it came his way nonetheless.

"It was so overwhelming," Jeff says. Of his many accolades, Jeff received the Calgary Emergency Medical Services' Citizen Recognition Award, the St. John Ambulance Life Saving Award for bravery, and the Governor General's Medal of Honour. He was also honoured for his efforts by the Canadian Olympic Association board of directors.

The day he was presented with certificates from both the fire department and Calgary EMS, Shannon Roberts was on hand to give Jeff her own personal thank you.

"He's the reason I'm standing here today," she told reporters, adding she had become the athlete's number one fan.

Awards for bravery weren't the only accolades presented to Jeff that year. "Through my diving I also got nominated for the sports athlete story of the year," Jeff says, adding with a smile that he didn't get *that* one. "The girl who won it swam across Lake Ontario and she doesn't have [full] limbs, and she swam all the way across, unassisted."

At the age of twenty-six, Jeff's life focused in a different direction. He married his sweetheart, Nicole, on 15 June 2002, and retired from his Olympic career in 2003—an experience that had taken him from Winnipeg to Edmonton, Vancouver, Calgary, and ultimately to Sydney.

He has kept in touch with Shannon Roberts and her fast-growing daughter. Several years after the accident, Jeff retains an affinity for the child whose life he saved before she was even born.

"The baby was fine—they've got a little three-year-old now," Jeff says, smiling at the thought of the little girl he'd seen occasionally. "Kennedy is her name and she's fine. Actually they stopped by our house for Halloween. She was wearing a little dinosaur costume. She's pretty cute!"

Jeff has a natural love for youngsters. He and Nicole had their first child, a girl named Carys, on 6 October 2005.

Jeff Liberty's life changed in other ways after the accident in the fall of 2001. After that fateful November morning, Jim took a job at a youth shelter, working with homeless and drug-addicted teens—a decision he said came directly out of his rescue experience. Later, he was one of eight applicants chosen from a pool of two hundred to work as a correctional officer at the Remand Centre in Calgary.

"When you're diving it's really hard to work, go to school, or anything like that," Jeff says. "I wanted to start getting a job where I could be proud of what I was doing."

For Jeff, life is one big adventure. He'll never again wake up and think he knows what to expect on any given day. He'll just ride the wave and see where it takes him.

Charlie Ellis with a tree swallow that is shopping for feathers. Charlie and his sister, Winnie, made a huge difference in the world of the birds near and on their farm. (Photo by Winnie Ellis, courtesy Ellis Bird Farm)

Charlie and Winnie Ellis

Mr. Bluebird

Some ordinary heroes *capture the limelight. Others, however, quietly perform their good works in the background, making important contributions to the world around us.*

Charlie and Winnie Ellis were a shy brother and sister who lived quietly on a farm in central Alberta, near Prentiss. One day, they made the simple decision to put up a nestbox in their yard, never knowing how that one action would change their lives and the lives of hundreds of others.

That one nestbox a half-century ago led to a groundbreaking partnership with industry that sparked the creation of the Ellis Bird Farm Ltd., dedicated to preserving not only the beautiful bluebird, but raising vital awareness of prairie wildlife in general. The Ellises didn't set out to become celebrities, but for lovers of birds and of the unique prairie environment, they were knights in shining armour, helping to preserve the natural balance of their corner of the province.

Charlie and Winnie Ellis were environmentalists long before the term was coined, but they only set out to save "their" birds, one nest at a time.

Charlie set up his first nestbox in the yard of the Ellis farm in 1955. To his delight, a pair of tree swallows quickly moved in. But

Charlie was horrified when a rival group of house sparrows soon overtook the nestbox and killed the swallows.

House sparrows are foreign to North America. They were brought to New York from England in the 1850s to devour insects; the birds soon spread across the continent. The European starling was another non-native species introduced to North America around 1890. By the time Charlie put up his first nestbox, the bluebird population in Alberta was declining due to habitat loss caused by industrialization and urban growth, and because of the influx of these two foreign species of bird.

After he discovered the dead tree swallow family, Charlie set up more nestboxes and was determined to keep the house sparrows away from his farm site so the feeder birds and the native birds that used his nestboxes had a chance at survival. Early each morning, he checked on them with pockets full of feathers for the tree swallows to use in their nests. Meanwhile, he used traps to eventually reduce the number of house sparrows.

"Whenever Charlie walked his bird trail, he would carry white feathers with him and the tree swallows would take them from his hat band or his hand. He said that he did this because the swallows liked to change their sheets," recalls Jennifer O'Brien of the Red Deer River Naturalists, past chair of the Ellis Bird Farm's board of directors.

Charlie and Winnie both became involved in helping the birds. Soon some mountain bluebirds also took up residence in the nestboxes. The Ellises were ecstatic, and the bluebirds proved to be good neighbours for the tree swallows.

Back in April 1852, Henry David Thoreau wrote in his journal, "The bluebird carries the sky on its back." He certainly wasn't the bird's first admirer. Songs have been written about the bluebird for years. It has long been a symbol of peace and hope and is still considered a harbinger of spring in North America.

"Bluebirds have long been appreciated by humans because of their beautiful colour and gentle nature," says Ellis Bird Farm biologist, Myrna Pearman.

<hr />

What started with one nestbox soon became a passion for Charlie, and before long he had three hundred nestboxes on his property, with more added each year. He and Winnie also began to feed wintering birds, using up to two tons of sunflower seeds each season. They bought cases of apples and raisins for their winged friends and also put out suet and peanut butter for them. Winnie even baked johnnycake for the summer birds. All native birds were welcome on the farm—juncos and other native sparrows, purple martins, mountain bluebirds, tree swallows, chickadees, blue jays, nuthatches, evening grosbeaks, redpolls, and woodpeckers—but not the house sparrow or the European starling.

No one really knows why Winnie decided to devote her life to helping her brother take care of the birds, says Myrna.

"She did teach for one year in Hanna, but found that it wasn't her calling," she says. "She cared for her parents in their old age and then stayed on to help Charlie with the farming operation."

Charlie worried over "his" bluebirds and tree swallows as well as the other native species that nested on his farm. He was vigilant about defending them from the sparrows and the starlings, as well as from cowbirds and predatory hawks. Once, when a mother bluebird had been killed by a house sparrow, Charlie took the six orphaned bluebirds and, one by one, placed them with other bluebird and swallow families in other nestboxes. He created his own bluebird adoption program.

"Do the birds know Charlie?" asked Bryan Shantz, the first biologist employed by the Ellis Bird Farm, in a 1986 article in *Omphalos* magazine. He recounted a story of the birds following Charlie for the feathers he carried. When Winnie wanted to take a photograph of the scene, Charlie put on a new hat and the swallows refused to come near him. They were used to the old hat and the new one scared them, so he had to put his old hat back on, and the picture was taken with Charlie and the tree swallow, perched on his hand.

"Do the birds know Charlie?" Shantz repeated. "I think so."

Charlie certainly knew *them.*

"He knew which of his houses were occupied and by which species, how many eggs had been laid, how many young fledged. I don't say that he named them, but he seemed to know them very well," says Jennifer O'Brien.

O'Brien and her late husband, Michael, one of the original signatories of Ellis Bird Farm Ltd., first met Charlie and Winnie in the mid-1970s.

"We found both of them welcoming, unassuming, with an amazing knowledge and appreciation of the environment and the world, and particularly of their own area of the environment and its inhabitants—especially the bluebirds and tree swallows, but also the other birds," Jennifer says.

"Whenever we visited, Winnie always had the coffee pot on and homemade sweets to go with it. Charlie would take us out to see the birdhouses he was building or repairing, or the latest gizmo he had made to keep [predatory] birds away from the bluebird and tree swallow nests."

Myrna says Charlie was a handyman who could make just about anything.

"Charlie wasn't one to go out and buy anything new," she says. "He was very creative at fashioning and manufacturing items out of materials at hand. Whether it was equipment repairs, tools, or house sparrow traps, almost everything he made was created from existing materials.

"His house sparrow traps were quite the complicated contraptions involving wooden pieces, wire, and metal taken from old licence plates."

Charlie would proudly show visitors around the bluebird trail on his farm. If they were in a car, he would walk in front of the car to make sure any fledglings were at a safe distance. Only a few years after building his first nestbox, Charlie was already becoming known throughout the province for his guardianship of the birds.

Although Charlie and Winnie avoided the limelight, they attracted the attention of local naturalist and author Kerry Wood, who in the introduction to his 1967 book, *A Time for Fun: A Guide to Hobbies and Handicrafts*, dubbed Charlie "Mr. Bluebird" in an effort to honour Charlie's contribution to the environment and role of protector of native bird species: "'Never mind my name,' says the man we call Mr. Bluebird. 'Just tell them how much fun it is to help the beautiful birds!'"

As time passed, and as Charlie and Winnie got older in the 1970s (both were in their seventies), they sometimes fretted about who would look after "their birds." Since neither had married, they feared there would be no one to inherit the farm when they were no longer able to care for it themselves. They knew their land would eventually be sold and divided up, and what modern farmer would be able or want to care for the birds the way Charlie and Winnie had?

The solution to Charlie and Winnie's problem surfaced in 1980 from an unexpected source, one that raised more than a few eyebrows.

⁓

In 1980, Union Carbide Canada Ltd. was looking for land near Red Deer to build an ethylene glycol plant. Ethylene glycol is a chemical used to make antifreeze and is a base for polyester fibres. The Ellis farm fit the bill nicely, and an offer was made to Charlie.

At first it sounded like the worst possible thing that could happen to the Ellis farm. Wouldn't a huge plant scare away the bluebirds? Was this the end of twenty-five years of providing a safe haven for birds? But what at first seemed to naturalists like putting a fox among the chickens (or, perhaps more appropriately, a sparrow among the swallows) turned out to be a blessing in disguise. The company was willing to buy the land but leave Charlie and Winnie to live out the rest of their lives in their home and to retain four quarter sections (called the Preserve Land) solely for agriculture and the bluebirds. Best of all, the company would help carry on Charlie and Winnie's legacy by establishing and giving arms-length support to a not-for-profit company to be called Ellis Bird Farm Ltd.

There was another stroke of luck. Walter Lindley was working in Montreal as Manager of Technology–Chemicals and Plastics for Union Carbide when he was told he would be managing the new plant in Alberta. But Walter was no ordinary chemical engineer. He grew up in England during the German bombings of the Second World War. Many children were evacuated to the countryside to avoid the destruction in the major cities, and Walter found himself in rural Leicestershire.

"I joined the Boy Scout movement and developed a great interest in birds and birdwatching," he recalls. "I was a member of the Royal Society for the Protection of Birds during my teenage years."

The new Union Carbide plant manager loved birds! Far from being an unwelcome part of the deal, Lindley found that becoming a corporate guardian for bluebirds was "a pleasant surprise." He felt he would have at least some common ground with Charlie.

What was his first impression of Charlie Ellis?

"[Charlie was] a very shy, retiring person who had a gentle sense of humour," says Lindley. "[He was] somebody who had a great love for his land and for all the things that go with that kind of respect.

He defended his point of view in a quiet but firm way. He knew his own mind and was not going to be overly influenced by his neighbours in the district. A kind and gentle man."

Walter once asked Charlie what the initials on his cattle brand, "MC," meant. "Why, it is 'My Critters,'" Charlie told him.

Lindley also remembers "his immense pride in the magnificent windbreak of both deciduous and evergreen trees on the west side of the Prentiss Road bordering his land. He was most concerned that enlarging the original road would damage the trees. I believe he put up those trees in memory of his parents."

Betty Lindley, Walter's wife, has her own memories of Charlie Ellis, particularly "his battered old hat, stuffed at the brim with feathers."

As for Winnie, Walter found her to be "a very intelligent lady, who would have made a superb teacher if she had grown up in other times," he says. "However, family pressures apparently did not allow it. She had a superb sense of humour and a love to tease—but never with malice.

"Her simple lifestyle had apparently changed little over the years up to 1980 and very little after that. She and her brother, Charlie, had lived in the same farmhouse for most of their lives. She was always up to date on what was going on in the local area, the county, the province, and Canadian national affairs."

So how do a chemical plant manager and a bluebird man become friends? "By showing an interest in what was happening on Charlie's farm and with the birds," Walter says. "[Being interested in] the mountain bluebirds or tree swallows, the state of the crops and cattle, and all that was going on in the local community. Also, [by] keeping both Charlie and Winnie up to date on what was happening at Union Carbide at the plant site at Prentiss and the progress on the building and operation of the plant, on a daily basis if necessary."

That's not to say Charlie blindly followed Union Carbide's lead. Even after construction of the plant began, Charlie made it known that he was still worried about the potential impact of the plant on his birds and on the environment of the farm, often wondering aloud if he'd made the right decision after all.

"In the very early days, when we were just getting to know each other, in an unguarded moment, I said to Charlie that people in this area seem to live to a ripe old age—it must be something in the air.

He shot back poker-faced, 'Yes! And we want to keep it that way!'" Walter recalls.

Ellis Bird Farm Ltd. was established as a not-for-profit company run by a ten-member volunteer board of directors. Charlie and Winnie were given lifetime memberships on the board, while representatives of Union Carbide, the County of Lacombe, Red Deer River Naturalists, the Federation of Alberta Naturalists, as well as four members-at-large made up the rest of the group. The mandate of the Ellis Bird Farm was to continue the work of Charlie and Winnie Ellis in not only preserving native bird species, but also in educating the public about conservation issues regarding them.

The board made sure it had qualified and talented staff overseeing the important aspects of operating the farm and its programs. Bryan Shantz, hired as the farm's biologist, promoted bluebird conservation by expanding the farm's bluebird trail, initiating banding and other research programs, networking with other bluebird trail operators across North America, launching educational programs, and publishing the first book on mountain bluebirds, *Mountain Bluebird Management*. He stayed with the farm until 1986.

Farm biologist Myrna Pearman began working with Shantz as a summer student in 1983 and was hired full-time at the farm in 1987. In 1984, she and Bryan co-wrote *Nestboxes for Alberta Birds* and, in 1992, she wrote *Nestboxes for Prairie Birds*, a book about native cavity-nesting birds.

Myrna recalls the first time she met the Ellises.

"I remember the smell of fresh-baked bread as I walked into the house and how both [Charlie and Winnie] were insistent that I join them for coffee," she says. "They were both shy people, and I knew that their decision to sell their farm to Union Carbide was made only after much soul-searching and deliberation. They were very concerned about the fate of their bluebirds."

Myrna saw the farm undergo dramatic changes during her first few years there. When she started, Charlie and Winnie were still living in the farmhouse, and her office was at the Union Carbide plant on the neighbouring quarter section. During her years working for the farm, she would see it change into the research and education centre it is today.

She learned very quickly how dedicated Charlie was to his native birds.

"I remember telling Charlie once that brown-headed cowbirds had laid an egg in a nest of a least flycatcher in what we now call the West Woods," Myrna says. "Charlie was surprised that I hadn't removed it, so he returned later that evening and spent hours searching the woods until he found that nest and removed the egg."

On another occasion, Myrna made a startling discovery.

"We kept Charlie's original boxes around the farm fencelines," she recalls. "I remember checking one of them and noticing pink insulation coming out of a hole that mice had chewed. When I inquired, Charlie explained that the birds had suffered during one early spring snowstorm, so that fall he removed all the boxes and retrofitted them with insulated walls!"

Finally, in 1980, the day came when Charlie had to hand over the protection of his birds to others, but he knew that, between Ellis Bird Farm Ltd., its volunteers, and Myrna, they were in good hands. Still, he continued looking after his birds until he passed away from cancer in 1990.

"I spent time with Charlie during his last days at the hospital, and once during our quiet time together he told me that he approved of what we were doing and that I was doing a good job. It was praise that I cherished," Myrna says, adding that the man's contribution to preserving the environment in Alberta shouldn't be underestimated.

"Charlie was instrumental in re-establishing mountain bluebirds in central Alberta," she says. "His farm supported what is believed to be the highest population density of mountain bluebirds ever recorded—they had about sixty pairs on their farm. He was also instrumental in inspiring others to build and set out bluebird trails.

"Mountain bluebirds would not likely have become threatened or endangered without Charlie's efforts, but his conservation program no doubt facilitated a local population increase. Most importantly, he was the inspiration to countless other people who now maintain bluebird trails in their own communities and neighbourhoods, and, because of Charlie, are actively involved in bluebird conservation."

Charlie's fears of losing his bluebirds because of the nearby chemical plant turned out to be unfounded. Based on data collected over twenty years, the presence of the plant in his backyard did not have a negative effect on the bluebird population in the area.

───────

In 1990, after her brother died, Winnie Ellis chose to move into a seniors' lodge in Lacombe. Afterwards, the board of directors for the Ellis Bird Farm decided it was time to share the farm with a wider audience. A visitor centre opened in 1995, replacing Charlie's old machine shed, and a core of dedicated volunteer gardeners spent hundreds of hours cleaning out Winnie's old gardens, which would be used to educate people on using native plants in their gardening.

Winnie continued to be a regular visitor to her farm, coming down every summer for as long as she was able.

"Winnie would walk through the gardens, admiring her flowers. She was happy to see that her gardens had been restored to their former glory, and that they were being enjoyed by so many people," said Myrna. Winnie passed away at the age of ninety-eight on 21 May 2004.

───────

Thanks to Charlie and Winnie Ellis, many people today enjoy increased awareness about mountain bluebirds. From the few dozen people who would visit each summer in the old days, the Ellis Bird Farm grew to the point where, by the mid-2000s, it was welcoming six thousand people every year, including as many as eight hundred school kids on summer field trips. Since 1988, the farm has offered a free off-site program called the Nestbox Program to encourage rural children to set out boxes and care for bluebirds.

"Because they can be so easily attracted to boxes, bluebirds have responded to grassroots conservation efforts," says Myrna. "There's not much the average person can do about polar bears or peregrine falcons, but with a few boxes placed in appropriate habitat, we can help the bluebirds."

The Ellis Bird Farm site today is a demonstration naturescape area, with butterfly gardens, xeriscape gardens, and hummingbird and water gardens. The farmyard is a living classroom where rural and city people can learn how to make their yards more environmentally friendly. There's a network of trails, ponds, and orchards.

Bluebird trail operators have donated nestboxes for display so the site now boasts the world's largest outdoor collection of bluebird boxes, about 228 different boxes.

The old Ellis farmhouse was transformed into a tea room in 1996, and once again the sweet scent of baking greets visitors, just as it did when Winnie was living there. It's as if her spirit is still tending the kitchen.

About 112 acres of the farm have been set aside as habitat preservation areas. The board of directors works with several partners to manage the farm as a demonstration conservation farm, and with technical support from the conservation group Ducks Unlimited, several wetland areas have also been established.

It also remains a working farm, says Myrna. "[We grow] canola, barley, peas, forage crops, [and] pasture," she says. "Our tenant farmer runs about one hundred to two hundred head of cattle each summer, depending on forage availability." This kind of environment is considered attractive to the birds as well.

The mandate of the Ellis Bird Farm is to carry out a summer nesting program and a winter bird feeding program, to conduct and support scientific research (as of 2005, the farm has banded about nine thousand birds), and to develop and deliver public education programs. The farm continues to be funded through an annual operating grant from ME Global (formerly Dow Chemical, which merged with Union Carbide in 2001), an endowment fund established by the Red Deer and District Community Foundation, private donations, and the sale of books and other items from the gift shop.

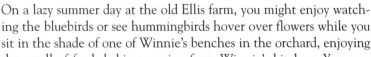

On a lazy summer day at the old Ellis farm, you might enjoy watching the bluebirds or see hummingbirds hover over flowers while you sit in the shade of one of Winnie's benches in the orchard, enjoying the smell of fresh baking coming from Winnie's kitchen. You may see kids on a summer field trip or people out counting butterflies.

Charlie and Winnie loved to have guests. They would be happy to know their farm is still such a welcoming place.

But most of all, you can wander along the bird trails and see for yourself that this one small piece of central Alberta has been preserved in the true spirit of the Ellises. Charlie and Winnie's bluebirds have a safe home here. With the determination of some very dedicated people, the Ellis Bird Farm will be a legacy for generations into the future.

Charlie couldn't have predicted this outcome fifty years ago when he put up the first nestbox in the yard of his farm. Can just two people make a huge difference? Remember Charlie and Winnie Ellis.

Robert Cardinal's mother Yvonne Cardinal, with mementos of her son's heroic deed—saving his wife and stepchildren from a burning building.
(Photo by Lisa Wojna)

Robert Cardinal

The ultimate sacrifice

The late afternoon sun casts long shadows on a cold, mid-January day as Yvonne Cardinal visits her son's grave on the Saddle Lake Reserve north of Edmonton. The tree limbs and shrubbery the sun uses to form these shadows move slightly with each sharp breath of winter air, giving them a life of their own, as if they're spirits dancing across the landscape. Robert Cardinal, just thirty-four years old when he died, lies buried next to his mosom, *which is Cree for grandfather.*

"I thought to myself, 'Dad, you came to pick up Robert, so you take care of him,'" Yvonne says as she brushes aside errant leaves and debris from the wooden cross marking her son's final resting place.

She last visited her son at the University of Alberta Hospital in Edmonton one late September day in 2003, the night before he finally succumbed to the injuries he'd sustained twenty-nine months before. She brought him his favourite meal: a submarine sandwich and a pop.

"The last thing that he told me . . . he said, my late father who died ten years ago came to visit him," says Yvonne. "He said, 'My *mosom* was here a couple of times.'"

"I said, 'Do you mean my dad?'" Yvonne remembers asking, concerned that perhaps Robert was experiencing some side effects or delusion because of his medication. "I asked, 'What did he say? Can you tell me?'

"And he said, 'Well, he told me a lot of things.'"

Robert wouldn't elaborate on this, promising Yvonne that he would tell her more the next day.

"He knew I was going to see him early in the morning because I was on my way to Hobbema for a Cursillo meeting," Yvonne says. "I wasn't going to go to that meeting, but [Robert kept telling me] to keep on with life."

The next morning, Yvonne was back in Saddle Lake and getting ready to drive down to Edmonton when the phone rang. It was her other son, David, with the news she had been dreading since the horrific fire more than two years earlier. Robert had died during the night.

"I don't remember much after that. My whole world turned black." Yvonne stops for a moment, choked by emotion that still, years later, threatens to overwhelm her. "Part of my world died, too. He was my best friend."

Standing by Robert's grave, Yvonne points out a new, granite memorial that will replace the simple wooden cross when the weather is warm enough to complete the task.

Robert's picture is centred on the stone, just above the word "hero," and below that his name, followed by the letters MB. "We can use those letters, you know—for Medal of Bravery," Yvonne explains.

The graveyard, located on a grassy knoll, is just west of the creek where, as a youngster, Robert spent many wonderful hours playing. Even as a young adult, he'd enjoy taking his nieces and nephews there to fish for whatever they might catch—or just to splash in the water on a hot summer day.

"He always loved going for a walk down the hill. It's beautiful down there, where he used to go," says Yvonne, glancing in the direction of the creek, a distant memory taking her back to a time when children's voices were raised in play, and the most difficult struggle she had was trying to mediate arguments between siblings.

"I never gave up hope. We were talking about him coming home because I was going to transfer him to Two Hills where there is a hospital. We would have done everything to bring him home."

It was after midnight on a warm Good Friday evening in April 2001. Everyone in the fourth-floor apartment on Edmonton's west side was asleep save for Robert Cardinal's wife, Anita, and her eight-year-old daughter, Harriet. The two smelled smoke and the fire alarm sounded. Seconds later, Anita found the front door and closet in flames that threatened to consume the rest of the apartment.

The rest of the family, including Anita's two other children and Robert, woke up, and it became clear that there was only one way out of the apartment—through the window. Robert and a neighbour grabbed a couple of mattresses and threw them down to the ground below. One by one, Robert gently lowered his wife and his stepchildren as far as he could before letting go. It was an incredible strain on the man since he had only one arm—he'd lost his right arm in a motorcycling accident years earlier. Anita, her three children, and one nephew made it out of the burning apartment safely.

But Robert Cardinal stayed behind in a frantic attempt to locate a second nephew, who was only ten years of age.

Several times, he returned to the window, gasping for clean, smoke-free air, before turning back to search the burning suite. The boy was nowhere to be found. In the confusion, Robert was unaware the youngster, who had been sleeping in front of the television, had already escaped the fire with only minor injuries.

Finally, Robert was unable to continue searching and rushed through the burning doorway. No one will ever know why he decided to enter the hallway rather than follow his family out the window. Perhaps it was adrenalin, or panic, or the thick smoke making it impossible for him to find any other way out. He was immediately engulfed by flames. When the firefighters found him in the third-floor stairwell, he was still burning. He was rushed to hospital, where doctors determined he had suffered second- and third-degree burns to ninety-three per cent of his body.

Yvonne was in Saddle Lake, preparing for that day's Good Friday church service, when she got the phone call notifying her of the fire and of Robert's injuries. By rights, Robert should have been visiting with her for the holiday, but that year Yvonne wasn't able to make the 160-kilometre trip down to Edmonton to pick him up.

"The next thing we knew, we were on the road and it was on the radio, on the news, everything," she says.

The authorities hadn't released the fire victim's name, but the news reports described him as a "thirty-year-old man in critical condition" and Yvonne knew by the description it was Robert.

"I was the first person to see Robert in the hospital," his brother David Cardinal says, adding that because he and sister Michelle lived in Edmonton, they were the first members of the family to be notified. "He was covered head to toe in bandages and he was swelling really badly. I couldn't believe this was my brother, and I had to ask to make sure they had the right person. I'll never get that image out of my mind."

When Yvonne finally got to the hospital, staff suggested she shouldn't go into Robert's room, but she insisted. And as she stood by his side—something she would do weekly, and sometimes daily, for the remainder of his life—she called his name, letting him know that she was there, and letting him know that she loved him.

"I assume he heard, but he was so out of it." Yvonne stops again, averting her eyes to nothing in particular while she toys with a piece of Kleenex, absently wiping the tears that flow with fresh grief. "From there on it was a long journey. He was in the hospital for twenty-nine-and-a-half months before he passed away. When you see your child in pain you wish it was you.

"He was badly burned, but he never gave up hope. He went through a lot of skin grafting—a lot of surgeries—right up to a few days before he died."

Most people don't survive this kind of injury. Robert's outlook for recovery was poor.

"They said Bobby had a fifty-fifty chance."

Although Robert didn't remember much about the tragedy, Yvonne always asked her son why he elected to stay behind in the burning apartment for so long.

His reply: "Mom, when something like that happens you just do it . . . if somebody died in that fire, I didn't want to be responsible."

During that first year after the blaze, Yvonne and Robert talked about the fire a lot, but eventually Robert didn't want to talk about his decision anymore. Instead, he wanted to leave the past behind and talk about what he'd do when he came home—how he'd build a fence for his mother, and how he'd visit the creek again and try out the fishing rod he had received the previous Christmas, which was now hanging on his hospital room wall.

"He never gave up hope. He never, never gave up hope," says Yvonne.

Still, the gruelling routine of daily dressing changes and regular surgeries wore even at Robert's patience.

"There were times when we talked about death," Yvonne says. "For a long time his feelings were up and down—times when he was afraid or times when he was happy. Most of the time, he was happy. I think his bad days was the times he was hurting so bad."

Adds his brother David: "One thing I admired is that he said he was glad if this did have to happen, he was glad it happened to him and no one else. He knew what pain and hell it was to live with those types of injuries he suffered, and still he was able to say that."

Anita, Robert's wife, had injuries of her own to deal with, along with the emotional scars that come with this type of tragedy. Robert struggled with not being able to see his wife and stepchildren more often, but his energies had to remain focused on getting well again.

For almost two years, Robert was confined to his bed, but for the last few months of his life he improved enough to spend some of his time in a striker chair, a specially fitted and designed wheelchair.

"It was amazing. After two agonizing years of this ordeal, Robert was finally able to sit himself up at an angle which would allow him to sit on mobile chairs," David recalls. "His skin was a bit more covered up and he wasn't at a big risk for infection anymore, so he was allowed to leave the confines of his room in the burn unit.

"This totally changed him. His emotional well-being increased a thousand-fold and he was finally able to enjoy life a little bit more. He loved to laugh, and with the worst behind him, we were finally able to laugh together."

The gift of a sense of humour was something Robert had in abundance.

"He would joke and tease innocently to promote good spirit and friendship, and he could take jokes himself and was never afraid to be humiliated. In fact, he thrived on it. He could laugh things off easily and people admired him for that," David says, fondly remembering one fun evening before the fire.

"Once we were watching a comedian in St. Paul and Bob stole the show away. He wasn't being a heckler, really, but he instantly forged a bond with the comedian and they took swipes at each other. They had everybody rolling with laughter. They dubbed him 'Sideshow Bob' that night. He was very good-natured about it."

About a month and a half before Robert died, he received a motorized wheelchair. It afforded him the chance to get outside from time to time without having to rely on his brother or mother to manoeuvre the heavy striker chair around the building.

"We spent a lot of time outside, him and I, because he loved being outdoors," Yvonne says.

Even as he lay suffering in his hospital room, his very survival for those twenty-nine months gave doctors a chance to learn much about burn injuries, and Robert was grateful that some good might come from his experience. Unfortunately, Robert's injuries were so severe that doctors were unable to save his legs, but even facing this, Robert agreed to try out some new medical techniques.

"Before doctors amputated his two legs, they tried using a new [Botox] treatment on his feet," David explains. "They were hoping that by relaxing the muscles in his feet he might regain some feeling to them, but that wasn't successful.

"He almost died a year before his eventual death, but in a last-ditch effort doctors administered a newly developed drug that was so powerful it managed to restart his failing kidneys."

That Robert gave so freely of himself wasn't out of character. David remembers how, as children, Robert took the role of the eldest quite seriously.

"One time in Saddle Lake, Michelle and Bob wanted to visit their Uncle Pete who was working at his confectionery store," David explains. "They were young and they used a bike to help them in their three-mile-long journey on a rough and gravel road with lots of hills. Bob would ride the bike up each hill and he would let my sister Michelle ride the bike down the hill. She told me this story, and she really loved him for that.

"It took them all morning to make it to the store and the funny thing was once they got there, Pete was on his way home for lunch so he picked them up in his truck and brought them home."

On another occasion, Robert and his siblings—David, James, and Michelle—devised a game whereby they'd roll crabapples down a side street onto a busy, intersecting roadway.

"I guess our objective was to see who could roll their crabapple across the street without having it run over by a vehicle—or it might

have been to see who could get the most spectacular apple explosion
. . . one of the two, anyways," David recalls.

"After angering some motorists, a few of them came chasing after
us. We fled in all different directions. James and Michelle were
nabbed immediately. I was so scared I kept on running . . . but
because my sister was crying and scared, Robert turned himself in so
he could comfort her."

Robert's resilience at battling his injuries strengthened his family—especially Yvonne and David—when the trips to the hospital
became draining.

"I couldn't see myself being in bed [all the time]," Yvonne says,
unable to hold back her tears. "But he used to say, 'Never give up on
life.' And I always asked him, 'Why do you say that?' and he said,
'You know if you give up on life you never become anything.' He
showed me courage. When I wasn't there, David was there during
the week. Every chance I could get I would go.

"I was getting to the point where I was burnt out. I was getting to
the point where I hated this hospital. And then I'd think after, when
I'd be coming home on the bus . . . I shouldn't feel like that. I'm
grateful that God gave me that time to be with my son—I think of
that now. You don't know your children until you're in that kind of
intimate setting."

And despite the pain, there was joy.

"We used to spend our Christmas, Easter, birthdays—we'd spend
all our celebrations in the hospital. It got to the point we had to haul
stuff (like turkey and all the trimmings)," Yvonne laughs.

"On August 23, 2003—that was a month before he passed
away—we had a big gathering, because all the kids were going back
to school. We just brought chicken and whatever we had, and then
we took him on a bus ride—we kidnapped him!"

From a medical standpoint, the nurses and doctors would have
likely discouraged such an outing. But from a spiritual well-being
standpoint, the kidnapping was an awe-inspiring experience.

"I woke [Robert] early in the morning—I knew he was sleeping
because he liked to sleep after his bandage change," says Yvonne. "I
said, 'Robert, get up, we're going now.'"

As Robert woke, he admitted he'd forgotten about their plans.
But it didn't take long before he was chomping at the bit to get on
board.

"So, I got him up in his chair—I had the nurses help me get him into the chair," Yvonne says. "My daughter drives an ETS [Edmonton Transit System] bus and she rented a bus with a lift.

"We took him all around Edmonton." Yvonne pauses for a second, then adds, "The nurses were looking for him."

Robert and his family were AWOL for two hours as they travelled around Edmonton. For Yvonne, it was a time of laughter and joking—a chance to forget, if only for a little while, the battle Robert was fighting.

"That was a good memory," says Yvonne.

Before the accident, Robert had dreams. He'd married in 1999, he had just graduated from a computer programming course, and he had been accepted as a full-time student at Edmonton's Northern Alberta Institute of Technology for the 2001 fall term.

Even from his teen years he had successfully fought against adversity, due to the loss of his right arm. "When he was fifteen or sixteen he was in a motorcycle accident," says Yvonne. Extensive damage to one main nerve in his arm resulted in an amputation. Although he was previously right-handed, Robert took the loss in stride and retrained himself to think left-handed.

David remembers his brother as wise beyond his years. "He shared his knowledge and experience all the time—especially when it came to the outdoors, about hunting and nature."

Investigators examining the cause of the fire that destroyed Robert's apartment and nearly killed him determined that an accelerant had been splashed on Robert's apartment door. It was arson.

Making the tragedy even more senseless, when the suspect was finally apprehended, Robert and his family learned they weren't even the intended targets. The culprit had set fire to the wrong building.

"What kind of a person would do that?" Yvonne asks, her eyes searching as if there must be a reasonable explanation somewhere. She wanted the charges against the twenty-nine-year-old suspect upgraded to murder after Robert's death, but the man was ultimately convicted of the lesser arson charge and sentenced to ten years.

On 27 September 2003, Robert lost his battle for survival. When Yvonne arrived at the hospital, she didn't want anyone escorting her into his room. She wanted a few moments alone with him. She had never really seen the full extent of his injuries until this moment.

"When he died, I had to see for myself . . . "

More than two years later, the memory of that day, of seeing his battered and burned body and realizing perhaps for the first time how much pain her son must have been in, is still overwhelming.

"The death hit me so hard. I've lost people in my family, too, but . . . losing my child, that's the hardest thing," says Yvonne. "I just couldn't bear it. I was getting to the point where I was depressed, crying all the time, but my family was so supportive.

"We're still hurting. We're damaged by it all. I know my children are not happy . . . there's a big hole in your life. For me, that's the way it is, but we have to go on. These are trials you go through, and now, after he passed away, I don't know if it made me strong—I don't know. Sometimes I feel strong. But sometimes when you're grieving you get so weak, you know."

For Yvonne, the grieving has not ended. The first place she frequently visits when making the trip from Saddle Lake to Edmonton is the University of Alberta Hospital where Robert lived out his final months. She'll visit the spots she'd roll his striker chair to so he could get at least a little fresh air. She remembers the hockey games she watched with her son and his favourite submarine sandwiches.

"I still feel his presence."

It's the same strong presence she felt when she made the trip to Ottawa in 2004 to receive Robert's Medal of Bravery from Governor General Adrienne Clarkson. Although it was awarded posthumously, Robert actually learned a year-and-a-half before he died that he would receive the award.

"We were supposed to go, him and I," Yvonne says. "He was happy and excited about it, but at that time he was so sick—he couldn't make it. He could never walk after the tragedy."

Every day Yvonne thinks of her son. Every day she remembers the newspaper articles, the hospital visits, the smile on Robert's face, his pain, his laughter. It's one way she tries to work through the grief.

But still, there's a life to celebrate. She reminds herself of Robert's admonishments—his insistence that life is wonderful and worth all the attention we can give to it.

She knows his spirit lingers and his soul is at rest.

And she knows that despite the tragedy, she and her family were truly blessed by Robert's life, his selflessness, his suffering, his pain, his hope.

For David, Robert's legacy is ongoing.

"He made me and so many others try harder to be better and more responsible people," David says. "He made us want to follow the examples that he led by—that performing good deeds are fun and rewarding, and we don't need to expect any compensation in return.

"Everybody agrees that Robert was a great and wonderful person, and what happened to him was an utter tragedy that happened through no fault of his own. His courage and bravery in staying behind to help others in the fire was an example of what a caring and loving person he really was. He really did deserve that Medal of Bravery—and we are all thankful to Canada for recognizing that fact."

Yvonne takes one last look at the picture of Robert on the granite headstone. What she feels is impossible to articulate. Still, there's some comfort knowing her son is home—that his spirit is freed from the pain of his physical body. Like the shadows cast by the early evening sun, Robert's spirit now wanders the rolling plains of his childhood home, along the nearby creek, around Uncle Pete's confectionery.

Yvonne will never know what secrets Robert's *mosom* told him before his soul departed. In her family, Robert's grandfather was considered an esteemed elder in a culture that has tremendous respect for their elders, and *mosom* was very much the patriarch of Yvonne's family. Standing in the graveyard, Yvonne knows Robert is there. She feels his presence. And she knows he is in good company.

Gordon Smith, the "Sock-it-to-me brother," amidst the mountain of socks he collects and distributes to Edmonton's homeless.
(Photo by Lisa Wojna)

Gordon Smith

The "Sock-it-to-me Brother"

Gordon Smith *was nicknamed the "Sock-it-to-me Brother" for calling attention to a necessity of life most of us take for granted. In fact, it's something we walk all over.*

Consider how much wear and tear our feet take every day. With every step we take, our feet exert as much as twelve hundred pounds per square inch of pressure. It's amazing our feet don't constantly ache and throb when we go to bed.

Now imagine yourself as a homeless person with no car and little if any money for the bus. You have to rely on your feet as your main, and likely only, mode of transportation. For these people, foot care is very important—but it's often the last thing that gets any attention. Opportunities to bathe are limited and chances to do laundry even more restricted, so it's not uncommon for homeless people to go without certain items of clothing, such as socks.

It was while attending a fundraising event for Junior Achievement in September 2003 that Edmontonian Gordon Smith first heard that a lack of socks for the homeless was a real problem.

"Someone made the comment that eighty-five per cent of the people that come to the Boyle McCauley Health Centre [BMHC] have no socks," Gordon says. The centre provides health services to many of Edmonton's homeless. "They have a foot clinic there, they have a needle exchange program, and a bath program. Lots of people who come there are homeless and suffer from diabetes or other health conditions, and they spend a lot of time on their feet, walking around. Many people [leave] the clinic with no socks even after their feet are treated because there are no socks available. Money is spent on other items with higher priorities.

"As a result of just hearing about this situation I thought, well, it can't be too difficult to get some socks."

Gordon, an instructor at Edmonton's Northern Alberta Institute of Technology (NAIT), approached some of his colleagues, asking if they'd be interested in donating a few pairs of socks. He also approached members of his Masonic Lodge (Acacia Lodge No. 11 GRA) for help, as well as students in the leadership program he was teaching at NAIT. Pretty soon, word of mouth grew until Gordon's sock collection grew into numbers even he hadn't imagined possible.

"I started to get some socks—like ten pairs, fifty pairs, one hundred pairs, that kind of thing," he says.

And he not only got socks, he got publicity. Before too long, reporter Cam Tait of the _Edmonton Journal_ wrote an article on Gordon Smith's sock program.

"Because I belong to [a] lodge, I called it 'Sock it to me, Brother,' because in the lodge we call each other 'brother,'" Gordon says. Tait's article, which ran on 28 April 2003, spurred interest in people wanting to know details about what he was doing and how they could help.

On one occasion, an elderly gentleman came to Gordon's house. The seventy-three-year-old retired man wanted to check Gordon out, to make sure he was legitimate. When he was satisfied that Gordon was sincere in his efforts, he committed to a donation of fifty pairs of socks each month.

"He was at one time homeless. Now he's in a position to give back to the community," Gordon explains.

Socks started coming in from other places, too. One friend from the Masonic Lodge celebrated his eightieth birthday with an open-house party and, in lieu of gifts, he asked people to bring socks for the Sock-it-to-me-Brother program, and ultimately donated some two hundred pairs to the cause. (Gordon himself later borrowed the idea for his own retirement party and collected another three hundred pairs.) Some of the students in Gordon's leadership course also took on the sock program as part of their community service work.

"We even have one lady who provides hand-knitted socks," Gordon says. "Another source has been some of the DATS (Disabled Adult Transit Service) drivers . . . and from their associated Muslim community they have provided me with some one thousand pairs of socks."

Media coverage of Gordon's program grew as word continued to spread. He was featured in local and national media, including the CBC television program *On the Road Again*, which aired a special episode titled "Even One Person Can Make a Difference" in February 2004. Other media covering the program included Edmonton's CHED Radio, and in April 2005, Gordon's program was profiled by Sally Johnson in the *Edmonton Sun*.

As more people learned about Sock-it-to-me-Brother, donations began to pour in. Manulife Financial recruited employees on all thirty-six floors of Manulife Place in downtown Edmonton to collect socks, an effort spearheaded by one of Gordon's former students. One ATCO employee, another former student of Gordon's, collected an additional sixty pairs.

"People were bringing me socks from all over the place. It was now almost self-perpetuating," Gordon says. As the program continued to grow, Smith inadvertently became the vessel through which others could give. At any given time, Gordon would have as many as four lockers at NAIT filled with socks, as well as packages of socks filling his office, his garage, and even the corners of his house. There were socks all over the place waiting to be picked up and distributed to BMHC and other organizations.

By the fall of 2003, the program had expanded to include donations of toques and mitts. Later, the Women's Emergency Accommodation Centre (WEAC), an Edmonton shelter, spoke to Gordon about the need for women's undergarments, another necessity often neglected by those in need, and he expanded his efforts to include a program to collect women's bras and panties.

"The bra program is more difficult because, me being male, I was not aware of the need," says Gordon. "I recruited a woman from Alberta Treasury Branches who supervises some ninety female tellers. The residents at WEAC will be the prime recipients of the bra program."

Word of the expanding sock program crossed the country and donations began to come in unsolicited. "I got socks all the way from
Nova Scotia," Gordon says. "And I got some from Manitoba and
some from Ontario."

Even media outlets covering the story got involved in more ways
than just spreading the word—they actively canvassed for donations. For example, the *Edmonton Sun* held a sock-collection drive at
its office that added to the fast-growing stockpile of socks.

Gordon may have been excited at the success of his efforts, but
Cecilia Blasetti, executive director of BMHC, was even more so.
Knowing many of the clients who receive the socks collected by
Gordon personalized the donation. Cecilia understood what many
people didn't—that the homeless and other clients of organizations
such as BMHC suffer from challenges far more complicated than
most of us could imagine.

"Our target populations are people who have multiple barriers in
terms of accessing traditional health care systems," Cecilia explains.
BMHC services about forty thousand Edmontonians. "They're homeless, they suffer from social isolation, there is a high population of
Aboriginal people, a high population of mental health and substance
abuse clients, poverty is epidemic, and most clients would be unemployed with very low education levels as compared with the general
population. Hardly anyone has just one of those issues—most people
have a big combination of all of them.

"For most of them, their main mode of transportation is walking—so they wear out socks. It's not like they've got a drawer full of
socks at home to change them and wash them. They're not washing
them all the time, their shoe wear isn't good, usually, and there are
high incidences of things like diabetes, which, if someone's feet are
bad with that, can really be a tragedy for them."

Cecilia says socks donated through Gordon Smith's program allow
BMHC to have clean socks ready to hand out if someone comes off
the street to use, for example, the centre's drop-in bath program.

She says many of the clients accessing the services of the centre
suffer from painful foot conditions. "Sometimes they just come in
and our LPNs [licensed practical nurses] see them and they soak their

feet—we give them clean socks. Sometimes that's all it takes; it's just really simple things to help them."

Sleeping on a park bench isn't a rarity for many of the clients accessing the BMHC, says Cecilia. Many clients struggle just to put some food into their mouths each day. Buying socks isn't a priority. In fact, anything they have to pay for is going to take a back seat to what they see as their daily necessities.

"Our people just can't pay for things," Cecilia says. Most people on the street, whether they're homeless seniors or prostitutes, are merely surviving—nothing more. Having a shower and clean underwear to put on are seen as luxuries. "One of our nurses brought up the idea of a sock-washing program. People turn in their socks and if they are in good shape they are washed and reissued."

Gordon says he's learned how important his donations are to the homeless.

"People's feet get scalded, the sweat creates a scalding effect, and summertime is actually probably worse than winter," he says. "They're on their feet all the time, and they don't wash their socks so if they get wet their feet could be wet for literally days and then trench foot sets in.

"Trench foot is a problem made prevalent in the First World War when soldiers were faced with long exposure to wet feet in the trenches. When left unattended, it leads to hideous sores, blisters, swelling, and sometimes gangrene and even amputation. Street people suffer from the same thing in various degrees of complication because they are on their feet and quite often damp. This condition is treatable if caught in time and under the proper care."

Thanks to the donations, there are plenty of socks to go around for clients of BMHC, to help reduce problems such as trench foot. Gordon estimates the centre goes through about two hundred pairs of socks each month.

"Since my program has been in operation, not one person has left the clinic without a pair of socks if they needed them," says Gordon.

Granted, not all the recipients of Gordon's socks are aware of the time and effort that went into collecting the donations. But they do know their feet are dry and warm—and the staff who work with these people on the hottest days and the coldest nights know there is less chance of someone losing a foot to disease.

Gordon Smith continues his efforts to collect socks despite facing his own challenges. A battle with spinal cancer in the 1980s left him confined to a wheelchair, so he was no longer able to physically deliver the socks himself. Instead, he acted as a liaison between donor and destination, collecting donations and distributing them to staff members who come to pick them up.

Gordon estimates he collected about eighty-three hundred pairs of socks and distributed about five thousand pairs in the first two years of the program. He prefers to dole them out sparingly so as to encourage recipients to wash and reuse their socks, rather than just throw them away.

Gordon's garage on the south side of Edmonton is testament to the success of the collection. Mountains of garbage bags stuffed with new socks line the walls, taking up all but the minimum space set aside for the family vehicle.

"I only take new socks," he says, opening one bag after another. Every once in a while he pulls out a hand-knitted hat and scarf set, or a pair of mittens. It's clear the project has given him much pleasure, but not because he sees himself as having accomplished anything special. Rather, the continuous kindness and generosity of so many people is visible proof that the world is a wonderful place indeed.

Gordon Smith is the epitome of the super ordinary hero. His work isn't going to change the world, but for hundreds of needy Edmontonians, his efforts mean they have a little comfort in their lives. That's heroic enough.

Shirley Tripp with Boo Boo at the laundromat. (Note the bull dog slippers.) For hundreds of people, home is where Shirley is.
(Photo by T. J. Georgi)

Shirley Tripp
Everyone's mom

The little girl who grew up in Nova Scotia's Annapolis Valley will never forget her mother's words: *"If all you have is one slice of bread, then you cut it in half and give the other half to someone else."*

Shirley Tripp's earliest memory of giving happened after one Christmas when she was very young. Christmas was the only time her family got any fruit, besides the occasional windfalls from apple orchards that arrived after a hurricane passed through.

"Those apples that are on the ground are free game for anyone to help themselves," recalls Shirley. "Mum and Dad and all of us kids would go gather these apples and we'd put them in wooden barrels in the cool room and that would be our fruit for the year. But at Christmastime we would get an orange or some grapes."

Those oranges were precious—Shirley would save hers until it was on the verge of spoiling before finally eating it. One day she took an orange to school and discovered that one of her friends didn't have anything for lunch, let alone a rare orange.

"She was all excited because I had an orange and she didn't have one," says Shirley, "so then I gave it to her."

This started a lifetime of giving for Shirley.

Shirley grew up, moved to Alberta, and became a member of Edmonton's business community, with a family and a successful business in suburban Mill Woods called the Millbourne Maytag "Just Like Home" Laundromat. She wanted for nothing, but remembered well her mother's words of advice.

From 1998 to 2005 she instituted an annual tradition of offering Thanksgiving dinners for the needy, transforming her laundromat into a place where Edmontonians could enjoy friendly company, kindness, and a good meal. That first year, only about fifty people took part in the event, but the dinner grew each year until, by the mid-2000s, Shirley was serving more than a thousand people.

Shirley became known as "the Slipper Lady" because she wore large animal slippers as she worked, including during the Thanksgiving dinners. The tradition started with a gift from her grandchildren years ago.

"One thing that is special to me is how I can get everyone to look at my feet and smile, no matter how hard things are for them or how depressed they are," she says. "I wander around with my animal slippers on all the time, and during these meals, and everyone looks at my feet and manages to smile."

To visit with the Slipper Lady was to be instantly welcomed like an old family friend and drawn into her world. The laundromat truly was her second home. Her three small dogs were regular fixtures at the place: Tasha, a dachshund who liked to bury herself under a blanket on a chair, Pippi, an elderly Shih Tzu always hiding under the coat rack, and Boo Boo, a cinnamon-coloured sweetie that was a "snoodle" (half-poodle, half-schnauzer) who followed Shirley around the laundromat. Each animal had its own bed in the store. Animals and people alike were drawn to Shirley like a magnet. Everyone called her "Mom."

The walls and shelves of Shirley's laundromat were decorated with antique homemaking toys like an ironing board and iron and an aqua-coloured washing machine. There were also antique laundry plungers and tubs on display, along with a clothesline of old-fashioned clothes pinned with old-fashioned clothespins. The walls were covered with framed newspaper stories featuring Shirley and her dinners and even a photo of her posing with TV's Maytag repairman, the late actor Gordon Jump of WKRP in Cincinnati fame.

Shirley's business and her Thanksgiving meals were true family affairs. Besides her husband, Don, she could also call upon her five children: Carl, Angela, John, Maureen, and Nicole, who ranged in age from thirty-three to forty-five. John and Maureen were helping out at the laundromat one day when an anonymous donor dropped off a box of perfect pears and another box filled with spotless containers of chopped-up melons. This was an almost daily occurrence at the laundromat, says Shirley. The donors knew these items would get to the people who needed them most. On this occasion, the fruit was immediately passed along to families waiting on the self-serve side to do their laundry.

Shirley's childhood in the Maritimes gave her a sympathetic perspective when it came to getting to know the people and the families who came to the laundromat each year for a hearty, home-cooked meal—very possibly one of the few they'd get all year.

"I know what it felt like when I was young to get a good meal. It was the most wonderful feeling to have a full stomach, which didn't happen too often," she says.

It's an irony of life that the people who often give the most are not the richest, but people who have been down that road themselves.

"I know that a lot of these people have a hard time, they've got big families and everything," Shirley says. "When they come through my door, you can just tell what the people are like. They can't even afford a candy for their child half the time. I give away more candies than I sell. The accountant's not happy with me, but that's beside the point."

It was her customers who inspired Shirley Tripp and her family to start the tradition of providing Thanksgiving dinners.

"I first started doing my Thanksgiving dinners in 1998 only feeding about fifty people, mostly boys from Newfoundland that had nowhere to go," says Shirley. Many young Newfoundlanders came out to Alberta to work in the oil patch. "They all pleasantly thanked 'Mom'; they still mostly call me Mom."

She and Don decided to continue the tradition and, by getting the word out through TV news spots, putting up signs, and old-fashioned word of mouth, soon they were serving more than a thousand people every year. People are drawn to a place of laughter, especially when they don't have a place to call home.

Many of Shirley's customers were low-income residents of apartments in the area, but the dinner attracted people from across the city.

"They are customers, lonely and just plain hungry from all over the city," says Shirley. "Everyone is and has always been welcome."

Most people get stressed out over having the extended family over for dinner. But what if your extended family consisted of a thousand people or more? Where would you start?

"It's all right down to a science now," Shirley says.

After years of experience, the Tripp "family" dinners for a thousand came to be planned with military precision. Shirley had it all memorized: the first step was to start with fourteen turkeys, two hundred pounds of ham, and almost a hundred pounds of roast. (Don't try *this* at home!) And that was just for starters.

Shirley fires off the routine:

"We go to St. Teresa's Church—they've got big walk-in coolers over there and ovens that will cook eight turkeys at a time—big turkeys. Don and I go in [and] he helps me to get everything into the oven, wash the turkeys, clean them, and then we go back in the afternoon and baste them.

"In the evening, we take them out of the ovens, and put the hams and whatever in, get everything cooked," Shirley continues. "Then we go to the church, put everything into the walk-in cooler so it'll stay cool till the following morning. Then [some] friends go to the church with Don and then they start slicing up all this meat."

Shirley takes a breath.

"The dressing I make a month in advance," she says. "We bought a deep-freeze that sits on our patio outside, just for Thanksgiving dinners. A month in advance, I plug it in and start putting things in it."

For dessert, the owner of a nearby cinnamon bun store often donated any buns that hadn't been sold, which also went right into the deep-freeze.

Shirley's not finished yet: "We [have] friends down in Nisku that do all our mashed potatoes for us. Our daughter's mother-in-law out of St. Paul–Mallaig makes all my cabbage rolls and perogies—she makes thousands of them." Shirley stops to take a breath. "In that case, it's not really that much work for us."

She's got to be kidding. It's not even Thanksgiving yet.

"The main job is just getting the meal served," Shirley says. "[If] you have canned vegetables, you borrow steaming trays from a restaurant. Within an hour, the food's hot in the steam trays. You come here at seven to eight o'clock in the morning, start setting the food up so come noon, it's hot."

Antique laundry tubs and laundry baskets were lined with plastic to serve the fresh buns. Shirley bought ready-mixed coleslaw and added the dressing the day of the dinner. And little things weren't forgotten either, such as the hundreds of restaurant-serving-size butter containers. The bakery staff at Sobeys, a local supermarket, always knew when Thanksgiving was approaching because they'd get an order from Shirley for a thousand fresh buns, for which they'd give her a discount.

All the tables in the laundromat are put to use. People even spilled over to the patio outside, so Shirley began erecting a large tent, eventually doubling its size to handle the larger crowds.

The Thanksgiving Day meals would start at noon and finish between three and four o'clock in the afternoon. The number of people served was tracked by counting the number of paper plates used.

It all sounds as if it ran like clockwork, but that doesn't mean that everything always went ahead without a hitch. Shirley gathered stories of her dinners around her like flowers in an often quirky bouquet.

About two hours before their third Thanksgiving dinner in 2000, Shirley and her two sons were preparing for the day. Suddenly, a man walked in and dropped a bag by the sink. Shirley could tell from the rattling that there were bottles in the bag.

"He then took another bag with him and went into the washroom," Shirley recalls. "A few minutes later, he came out of the washroom only wearing an orange garbage bag with holes cut in it for his arms and head to go through. He then put everything he owned into the washer and went into the washroom using up all of the paper towels and had a bath.

"I prayed that he would be done and dressed before all of the people came to eat. Thank goodness he did and then we made him an early plate of food, which he thanked me over and over for, and left."

In order to serve so many people in such a short time, Shirley banned smoking at the dinners. Smokers, she said, tended to eat their meal and linger too long over a cigarette. She had to keep people moving in order to give everyone a chance to receive a meal. People used to be able to go back for seconds, but such was the demand, Shirley had to begin limiting people to one big plateful each.

"We have people that completely abuse it," she says.

A painful memory crops up, though thankfully, she doesn't have many painful memories of her dinners. One year, a woman who was there with her two adult sons was busy dumping large quantities of food into containers she'd brought along.

"Can't you finish your lunch?" Shirley asked her.

The woman replied, "Oh, no, we already got what we want, we're just taking this home."

Shirley gently said: "Well, you know, we're going to start running out if I'm not careful how much we feed each person. I don't mind if you have a couple of plates while you're sitting here but it's not really fair to take it home."

The woman swore at Shirley, then told her adult sons to dump the food in the garbage.

"My whole body was vibrating," Shirley recalls, still shaken by the memory. She knew Don was busy on the other side of the laundromat and couldn't help. There were also many good-hearted people who were there just to help serve, and many more who were very grateful for the meal they were eating. She had to keep her composure.

"I didn't want any of these people to see me upset. And I was just shaking when I came around the other side," she says.

But something in the universe is looking out for Shirley Tripp. No sooner had that unpleasant moment passed when something else happened.

"This man comes in—his name is Iher; he owns a business. He comes up to me and he says, 'You're the girl I'm looking for, the Slipper Lady,' and he opens up my hand and he puts a thousand dollars in it," says Shirley. "I said to Don, that makes up for anything terrible that did happen."

Unfortunately, the thoughtless actions of some meant that others were unable to enjoy a meal that year.

"Later on in the day, we had to say to people, 'I'm sorry, we've run out of food,'" says Shirley. "We had a lot of people who were wanting to eat and there was nothing left for them because of these people that abused it." She later introduced ink hand stamps to make sure everyone had a fair chance.

Fortunately, Shirley's positive memories outnumber the bad. She loves to tell the stories of two people in particular. During preparations for the second annual dinner, Shirley appeared on television telling people about the free Thanksgiving meal.

Shirley recalled an elderly gentleman of seventy-five or eighty years of age who came by the laundromat before the meal, loaded down with tomatoes.

"I saw you on television, sweetheart, and you're just as beautiful in person as you are on TV," he told her. "I just want you to have these tomatoes for your dinner." Then he added, "I'm always going to remember you."

Shirley replied: "You know what, sweetheart, I'm always going to remember you, too!"

Another memory, another dinner: "[One] year, this lady was standing there and she looked so depressed and so down, standing in line, and she just kept on staring at me," says Shirley. "I went up to her and I said, 'What's the matter, sweetheart?' She says, 'I've just lost my job. I don't have any family at home, I can't afford a Thanksgiving dinner. I can't afford hardly anything right now, let alone a Thanksgiving dinner. This beautiful music and all these friendly people around—this has just made my day.'

"She just kept on saying, 'Thank you so much, thank you so much.'"

Shirley tried to make the meals entertaining as well as filling. Up on the raised office area at the front of the laundromat, she would often have a live band playing. One group she used for several years was called Baby Boom, whose members dressed like the Blues Brothers, complete with violin cases and sunglasses; later in the show they would do a wardrobe change and perform Elvis songs. They also did a tribute to Marilyn Monroe, and Shirley still has a photo of Don posing with "Marilyn." Don once brought them in to celebrate Shirley's sixtieth birthday and they sang Louis Armstrong's "What a Wonderful World," bringing her to tears.

Shirley's Thanksgiving dinners started out for people in her own
community, but soon word of the event had spread all around town,
to the point where homeless people were willing to hop a bus to
Edmonton's southeast to get to the laundromat.

Some people even drove in from Cold Lake, nearly three hundred
kilometres away. Shirley wondered how they got the money for gas
if they couldn't afford a Thanksgiving dinner. One of her daughters,
Maureen, pointed out that people didn't come just for the meal, but
for the companionship: "It shows they don't want to be alone."

For Shirley, all the hard work and occasional frustration were
worth it when she met people who truly appreciated the meal,
"when they stand with tears in their eyes thanking us or the stories
they tell me about not having a meal if it wasn't for the fact that we
did this," she says. "Or the ones that can't afford the bus to go back
home so I give them bus money. This is what makes me feel good
and want to continue helping people."

Shirley became a Thanksgiving media celebrity around town
because of the news broadcasts that regularly checked on the
progress of her dinners each year. Eventually, she found herself helping the less fortunate in another way.

On Christmas Eve 2004, Aon Reed Stenhouse, the insurance
brokers, gave Shirley the food donations their employees were collecting for the underprivileged. They told her they would drop the
food off at the laundromat, and Shirley pictured receiving maybe a
couple of shopping carts' worth of food. She was floored when they
brought in more than two thousand food items, completely covering every spare inch of the laundromat.

"You should have seen it—it was unbelievable," she remembers.
"Every table in the whole laundromat was loaded down with food.
All of a sudden customers started pitching in, helping me to do food
hampers. And I said, 'My God, Don, what do we do—who do I send
all this stuff to?'"

Shirley knew all her customers by sight but she didn't know
where all of them lived. Christmas was coming so she decided to
make hampers so people would have a good holiday meal. She called
Global TV Edmonton, a staunch supporter of her work that had
awarded her the title of Global TV's Woman of Vision for December
2004, and told them she had to get all the hampers delivered before
Christmas. They aired a segment about it right away.

"The next day the phone wouldn't stop ringing. You needed an answering service," she says. Don was put to work taking messages.

Shirley called Constable Rick Cooper, a neighbourhood police officer. He was there the next morning and insisted on delivering the hampers himself. He took Don's list. "He called the houses to say it was him, and he wasn't there to arrest them, he was there to bring them the food," says Shirley. In total, Rick delivered fifty hampers on his own, while another thirty were picked up by families.

Shirley also decided to host a lunch for the public on the Sunday before Christmas. Unfortunately, a fierce windstorm blew in the day of the event, blowing a portable sign advertising the lunch across the parking lot, and many people stayed home waiting for the food hampers to be delivered. As a result, fewer people than expected turned out. Rick Cooper, his wife, and others made up lunches with sandwiches and fruit—and he delivered those to people as well.

"He is one heck of a beautiful man. I just think the world of Rick," Shirley says.

The 2004 Christmas lunch didn't start out with pleasant memories. A few days before the lunch, someone broke into the Tripp home and stole most of their Christmas presents. The couple who gave so much to others had been heartlessly robbed. Gifts for the kids and grandkids were gone, Shirley was missing some of her family jewelry, and Don was missing his pocket watch. Their home had been ransacked.

To make matters worse, the donation can for the dinners was also robbed—not once, but twice. The money hadn't been counted yet, so it's not known how much was stolen.

But on the day of the lunch, 19 December, people flooded into the laundromat with gifts—for the Tripp family this time—chocolate, plants, hundreds of dollars in cash and cheques, and even a large bottle of Irish Cream to replace one that had been stolen. The Tripps were overwhelmed. Shirley, being Shirley, quickly and quietly donated much of the money to other causes.

Why would Shirley Tripp devote so much time to helping the needy, spending hours setting up dinners, putting up with the (occasional) ungrateful soul, and even donating money given to her after her family was robbed?

Don's reply is to make a tongue-in-cheek circular motion around his ear. Is he implying that she could be crazy?

"I *know* she is," he says.

Shirley laughs and replies, "He's helped me for years," implying that if she is crazy, then Don has one foot inside the asylum, too.

Don's pride in his wife's accomplishments goes without saying. He maintains a video archive of newscasts about his wife.

Shirley's daughter, Maureen, was asked why she thought her mom dedicated herself to the dinners every year. "To make people feel like they have a home," was her reply. "Everyone calls [her] Mom."

Shirley Tripp really is the mom that all of us dream about. That was probably why so many people reached out to her, donating their time, money, and food to help with her dinners. Her face lit up when she heard "thank you." It was addictive, and you wanted to see those blue eyes shine with happy tears and feel the sunshine of that smile again and again.

Global TV news anchor and Woman of Vision producer Lesley MacDonald, a long-time supporter of Shirley Tripp, admits she adores the Slipper Lady.

"With warmth and disarming charm, Shirley Tripp epitomizes the spirit of Maritime generosity," says MacDonald. "Just thinking about her makes me smile, the way she gives others a lift in their day watching the little lady with the big slippers strolling down the aisle of her laundromat, making sure everyone is taken care of.

"Whatever she has, she gives, and it's obvious she gets back ten-fold with a smile, a hug, or even in the heartfelt knowledge of knowing she has made a difference, even in some small way, in someone's life. Along the way, she inspires everyone she touches to give of themselves. She is a very special lady."

Shirley and Don often worked ten- to twelve-hour days, seven days a week—all this after Don retired from his job as a locksmith with the Edmonton public school board. But by 2005 it was time for Mom to take a break. They put their laundromat up for sale and new own-ers took over the business on 27 June.

"I'm going to miss it. But I can't stay forever," says Shirley.

That doesn't mean Shirley plans to retire from giving. Before the "For Sale" sign had even settled on the window, Shirley was already thinking of setting up a school hot lunch program. She'd seen far too many hungry kids in her lifetime. She hopes to continue the Thanksgiving Day dinners, though she doesn't know where or when. Meanwhile, the new owners of the laundromat kept the tradition going their first year, and their first Thanksgiving Day dinner in October 2005 served nearly a thousand people.

"I believe that while we're in this world, as long as we're doing something to help somebody else or doing something good, God's going to let us continue living," says Shirley. "But when we're *done* doing what we're here for, when we're done helping people, and we just sit in the corner and do nothing anymore, it's time to go. It's over."

For Shirley, it's not over just because she sold the laundromat.

"I've got too many things to do. I've got to do something else."

For Shirley Tripp, there really is no such thing as retirement—unless a person can retire from her own giving nature.

"That is what makes me the happiest, just to hear someone say 'thank you' and know I have helped in some small way," she says. "We all know we're going to die. So we all have a purpose here on Earth. No matter what the purpose is, we've all got something we should be doing."

Walden, left, and Art Smith enjoying a rare, quiet moment.
Two brothers, one mission: make a difference in someone's life before
the sun sets each day. (Photo by T. J. Georgi)

Art and Walden Smith
Two hearts of gold

It is easier to make an appointment to see the premier than it is to set up an interview with Art Smith of Wetaskiwin. You might think that Art is a thirty-year-old executive running a demanding business, but the only thing he has in common with one is the hectic schedule. After all, Art is eighty-four years old!

What's even more amazing is that he is the *little* brother of a two-brother team that has wowed Wetaskiwin for years with the unselfish gift of their time. Walden Smith, Art's brother, is *ninety-two* years young.

As you walk in the door of Art's house, you immediately notice the bags of bagels to one side (they will play a part in our story later). Art has just come home; his car overheated on the way back from Edmonton on a trip to take a local man to his cancer treatments. Art has driven the man there for the last ten days in a row, minus the weekend, and this will also play a part in our story. Very soon there is a knock on the door; big brother Walden has jumped in his car and driven over for the interview.

Art and Walden are at the age when many seniors have long since given up volunteering in order to enjoy a far less hectic pace—yet something drives them to keep on, to fill almost every day with service to others.

Art and Walden's volunteer work is woven so smoothly into the fabric of their lives that it's hard to tell where one aspect ends and the other begins. Helping is as much a part of them as eating is for the rest of us.

In fact, giving has become virtually a ritual for the brothers. Every day, Art, Walden, and four couples pick up bagels, doughnuts, and muffins from Tim Horton's, Safeway, and Grandma Lee's. And, twice weekly, Art and an assistant pick up soup and bread from the Wayside Inn, a hotel and restaurant.

This food is destined to be delivered to some fifteen needy families around Wetaskiwin.

After eight years of doing this, the brothers have the routine down to a science. First, they take the food to the local United Church kitchen and scoop the soup into medium-sized Ziploc bags donated by the Sobeys grocery store. Everything is then immediately put into a deep-freeze to await delivery.

"The soup comes in containers, three bags for one container; each bag does three bowls of soup so one container will have nine bowls of soup," says Art. "We average about six containers twice a week."

The number of families helped by the brothers' rolling "soup kitchen" continues to grow.

"We keep adding families," says Art. "Someone will phone and say there's a family I know that needs it."

The brothers admit that a number of the families they visit have major problems, and this has sparked the occasional disparaging comment from others.

"People would say, 'I bet the ashtray was full of cigarette butts and they were staggering to the door,'" says Walden. "That's the kind of stuff we get."

In fact, Art and Walden experience quite the opposite—people are pretty happy to see them.

"Oh sure, sure—if the dog doesn't get you first," Art adds. He and Walden laugh at their inside joke. There is one house with a loud dog, but Walden shrugs it off.

"The dogs are the messengers," Walden says. That particular family hears the dog barking and goes to the door to let Art and Walden in, he adds. It works better than a doorbell.

Recently, Art recruited Doug Klause, a former student, to help with carrying the heavy soup containers from the restaurant to the car. The realities of aging are not lost on the brothers. Art has a sore back and Walden now has some trouble with his legs, so they compensate by having friends give them a hand from time to time.

"Whenever the spirit moves us, we go around town and we take this stuff, pile a bunch of it in cars and go knocking on doors and give it to the people," Walden says.

"It isn't knocking on doors," Art corrects him. "We know what doors we're going to—we know where we're going."

Those who benefit from the food donations include single-parent families, low-income and unemployed families, and families receiving Assured Income for the Severely Handicapped (AISH) benefits.

Besides all the food, the brothers also bring books for some of the families.

"People give me books and then I take them to the various places around town . . . to the hospital, to the seniors' homes," Walden says. He always has a stack of books at home ready to give away—everything from novels to *Reader's Digests*.

One man told him, "You know, I can't read," so Walden didn't give him any. The next time Walden saw him, the man said, "Hey, Wally, give me some books." He wanted some to give to his friends.

Says Walden: "Nowadays, when Art and I go to take out food, we take a shopping bag and we put in there a loaf of bread, some soup, some doughnuts—What else do we put in there, Art? Lately I've been putting in there a couple of *Reader's Digests*. If they've got little kids, I go to the Salvation Army store and buy a bunch of books and then I put those kids' books in along with the doughnuts."

Food and books aren't the only items Art and Walden collect for the needy. For example, there's the eyeglasses.

"I buy glasses from the Army and Navy [store in Edmonton, at a] dollar per pair, and then I give them away," Walden explains. "Sometimes people will stop you on the street and want a pair of glasses. I've had that happen twice."

Eyeglasses are expensive, and many seniors living on fixed incomes simply can't afford to buy new ones.

"Hearing aids is what they [really] can't afford," Art says. A simple hearing aid can cost fifteen hundred dollars.

The brothers haven't tried to provide hearing aids for people (yet), but they are constantly listening to what people need in the community. For example, Art has been driving people to doctor's appointments since 1985, ever since he retired as a teacher. Wetaskiwin is a small city, and for some medical procedures, patients have to travel seventy kilometres to Edmonton, which can be difficult for those without a vehicle or the ability to drive themselves.

"You want to go to Edmonton to see the doctor or something, get Art Smith, he'll do it," Walden says, laughing.

Right now, Art is driving one person to Edmonton for cancer treatments. You might think these trips would be very depressing for Art. "Actually, I enjoy it," he says. "See, I'm selfish. I do it because I love it."

Art works with the local Family and Community Support Services (FCSS). They have a list of drivers to transport people who can't get to facilities in Edmonton on their own. Drivers also take people to appointments in Camrose and Red Deer, as well as short trips in Wetaskiwin. Although Art had recently asked to be put on the bottom of the list—all his other good work takes up so much of his time—often he is still called twice a week, or sometimes for five days in a row, or even more, as is the case with the cancer patient he has driven ten days running. Sometimes people specifically ask for him.

Walden often comes along on the Edmonton trips. The brothers are good company for each other.

"We argue. We never get mad at each other but we argue," Walden says.

"We agree to disagree," says Art. "Well, not if there's somebody else in the car. We get some pretty lady in there and Walden forgets all about arguing." He says his brother has always been pretty good with the ladies. Still is.

But we've still only scratched the surface of the brothers' volunteer work. Suddenly, in mid-sentence, Art stops to ask:

"By the way, want to come to a ham supper?" He's selling tickets to one of the main fundraisers for the United Church's men's group, AOTS. There are about twenty-five AOTS members in Wetaskiwin—including, of course, Art and Walden—but what does AOTS stand for?

"When we started up, we were a bunch of farmers basically and we were going to get a name for our group so we didn't know whether to use wheat, oats, or barley [in the name]," Art says. "Then

they said, 'AOTS? You got it spelled wrong!' Yeah, I'm sorry, we don't
know how to spell.

"It really means, if you read your Bible, "I am among you . . . "

" . . . As One That Serves," Walden finishes. "Art didn't want me
to tell you that until he got in his story about the oats."

The AOTS suppers are a twice-yearly event in Wetaskiwin. They
routinely host three hundred people for each supper (in November,
it's ham; in February, it's beef) and people line up patiently for their
turn to sit at the tables in a side wing of the United Church with a
kitchen, a stage, and a large seating area. There's not much elbow
room but no one complains. There's good food, lots of it, and pie to
die for.

The men do the cooking but admit they let their wives do the
scalloped potatoes and the pies. One year, they made chocolate
meringue, lemon, raisin, apple, blueberry, and pumpkin pies.

The suppers began about thirty years ago when the AOTS members were asked to put on a meal during the North Am snowmobile
races that used to be held in the Wetaskiwin area.

"The first year we had seven hundred [people]. And now we only
serve around three hundred," says Art.

Through AOTS, Art and Walden have also been involved in
donating money for building a women's shelter, schools, wells, and,
in late 2003, providing lighting in communities in the Dominican
Republic through the Add Your Light Charitable Foundation. Some
of AYL's work includes providing light-emitting diode (LED) lighting
(see the chapter on Dave Irvine-Halliday for more on this innova-
tion), bio-sand filters for purifying drinking water, McKelvie-
designed classrooms for adult night classes, a welding shop, and
other projects, says Art. He said this is just one of several projects in
which AOTS is involved. They also give money for scholarships, the
Red Cross, and church youth groups.

And it's not just Art and Walden who give their time to help others. Art's wife, Madeline, has about fifty-five years of volunteer work
under her belt, including forty years with the Red Cross and twenty-
five years working with Meals on Wheels.

Walden leaves the room for a short break, and Art brings out a couple of the awards he's received. The awards are not on display. One

that Art received from the Canadian Red Cross Society in May 2002 reads:

> Order of Red Cross member, in recognition of deep and abiding devotion to the fundamental principles of the society as exemplified by the extraordinary contributions made to our humanitarian work and in appreciation of ongoing commitment to the community.

"I've been organizing the Red Cross canvass for eighteen years," Art explains. "We [the Wetaskiwin branch of the Red Cross] were one of the top ten collectors in Alberta for quite a few years. I used to have one hundred and thirty canvassers and we raised twenty-five thousand dollars in the early years. Last year we raised fourteen thousand dollars because we only had forty-one canvassers. This year [2005], we only have twenty-five canvassers."

It's getting harder and harder to get people to knock on doors even for a good cause.

"We had a meeting and they said, 'Smith, if you quit, we're quitting,'" Art says.

Art himself is not averse to doing some legwork.

"I've got to do fifty businesses I'm canvassing right now before the end of the month," he says.

Another award Art shows is the 2000 Governor General's Caring Canadian Award, "in recognition of your outstanding and selfless contributions to your community and to Canada." Art and Madeline were invited to Ottawa to receive the award.

"She was my favourite gal after that," Art said of then-Governor General Adrienne Clarkson. His Royal Highness, Charles, the Prince of Wales, was also at the ceremony.

The trip was a high point in the life of a man who doesn't seek recognition. A lifetime of modest giving suddenly overcomes him and he quickly puts the awards away.

"I don't like showing them. Enough of that. Enough of that," he says, changing the subject.

But most of Wetaskiwin know the brothers and what they do. They often only have to show up at a store or the farmer's market and people approach them with offers of food and other donations.

Their reputation goes beyond Wetaskiwin, too. Just ask Glenn Smith, one of Art's four children.

"I was working in Carstairs," Glenn says. "I went to the United Church one morning and I said, 'Yeah, my name is Smith and I'm from Wetaskiwin.' And these people started going, 'Smith, Smith. There are two brothers . . . two brothers.'"

Why do these brothers give so much of their time to make the world a little bit better?

"I was born that way. I was born to volunteer," Art says.

Walden's favourite quote on the subject is from Stephen Grellet, a Quaker missionary from France who lived in the United States until his death in 1855: "I expect to pass through this world but once. Any good, therefore, that I can do or any kindness I can show to any fellow creature, let me do it now. Let me not defer or neglect it for I shall not pass this way again."

———

Charity was taught to the Smiths at an early age. There were eight children in the Smith family, and their parents had a great influence on them. Rev. Horace Greeley Smith was a Methodist minister who served Alberta in the early half of the twentieth century. His wife, Evelyn, was also a strong role model for her children.

"A preacher's wife was tied into many, many things in a small community—this along with all the work of feeding and caring for all her family," says Art. "She was expected to be a leader in the Ladies' Aid, to get all her kids to church on Sunday, and to bring up well-behaved kids."

Of his father, Art says, "Being a minister, he'd give everybody anything." Sometimes, his family was very happy to receive, as well.

Art and Walden tell the story about their dad and the "Bennett coat." One day, Rev. Smith had the honour of escorting the moderator of the United Church to various churches around Red Deer with a horse and cutter in 1932.

"It was a heck of a cold day, maybe thirty below, and my dad didn't have a very good coat," Walden recalls.

When the moderator got back to Ottawa, he told his good friend, Prime Minister R. B. Bennett, about the poor preacher out on the cold prairie without a decent coat. Bennett sent Rev. Smith a fur coat.

"So we called it the Bennett coat," says Art.

But it's a story that their mother, Evelyn, told that Walden remembers best. It may sound familiar to anyone who was a Boy

Scout. One day an old lady waited to cross a street. It was cold and icy, and she hesitated. A group of boys ran past her.

"And finally one boy stopped—I can't even tell it now," Walden says, tears coming to his eyes. "He stopped and he helped her across the street and then she went on, you know, and that night when she prayed, she prayed that the Lord would bless this boy."

Walden takes a breath and Art explains, in a whisper, that his brother is awfully soft-hearted. Walden continues:

"Anyway, that's the kind of story she used to tell us, stories about how people helped others. We wanted to be like that boy that helped the old lady across the street. And that was our philosophy: help others. So that's what we've been doing all our lives, Art and I, and the rest of the family."

The Methodist Church liked to move its ministers every three years, so the Smiths saw a lot of Alberta. Walden, the oldest, was the first baby born in the town of Chinook, located between Hanna and the Saskatchewan border. It was 1913, and the railroad had just come through. Over the years, the Smiths lived in a variety of towns: Elnora, Jarrow, Red Deer, Bowden, Millet, Carmengay, Veteran, and Mayerthorpe. By the end of their travels, there were eight children: Walden, Margaret, Mildred, Edith, Lloyd, twins Harold and Art, and Clarence.

Each Sunday, the children would sit in the first pew right in front of their father, who was giving the sermon.

"We always had to behave ourselves, didn't we, Wald?" Art asks.

"Oh, yeah," Walden replies.

Walden in particular had trouble keeping still. Rev. Smith would often stop right in the middle of his sermon. "My dad would say— 'Walden! Behave yourself!' I'd be wiggling around, you know."

But the kids got their revenge.

"We'd embarrass him," Art says. "You know the song, 'When the Roll is Called Up Yonder'? We'd sing, 'When the Romans called up yonder.'"

That sense of fun and mischief hasn't dimmed one iota over the decades. Back then, they were called "PKs"—preacher's kids.

"That means you're the wildest kid in the country," Art says. He's only joking, of course, but the combination of the constant moves and being preacher's kids probably made the five brothers and three sisters closer than ever.

"When we were kids, we'd just learned to skate and we didn't have any hockey sticks," says Art. "For Christmas, Walden got us [Harold and me] a couple of hockey sticks and we became famous hockey players after that. No, we did! We played a lot of hockey." The boys played for local teams and were well known for their skill.

Walden proudly remembers Art's skill with a hockey stick. "Yeah, they were good hockey players. Art was quick! He was just like Gretzky, you know. He'd dodge around the other guy and bang!" Another goal.

"He likes to lay it on a little," Art says.

Walden chose a helping profession like his father and became a teacher. He met his wife, Florence, when he was teaching in Sunnybrook, sixty-four kilometres west of Leduc. They were married in 1936. She was, and still is, the love of his life.

"She was the most beautiful young lady you ever saw," he says.

They couldn't afford much of a house. Walden's salary was only five hundred dollars a year, so they bought a former granary to live in.

"When you fall in love and want to get married, what are you going to do?" he says. "Our house cost us seven dollars and fifty cents. Wasn't that something?"

They lived in it for ten years. Art and Harold would often drop by for a visit.

"We used to have a houseful," Walden says. "Imagine that small place—it was eight by twelve, so the father-in-law built us another one, eight by twelve, so we had eight by twenty-four—and we used to have a house full of people. We had people like you can't believe."

It was at that little house in Sunnybrook where Walden remembers one of the first times that he and Florence really helped someone. A family with ten children lived nearby. Early one Sunday morning, there was a knock on the door.

"Here they were, about five of those kids, wanted to come in; wanted some breakfast, I guess," remembers Walden. It was the Dirty Thirties and this was a struggling, immigrant farm family. Walden says such families had it especially tough during the Great Depression.

"So we took them in and gave them some breakfast. Anyway, the next Sunday morning—bang!—knocking on the door again. So we did that for awhile and finally we just . . . " his voice trails off. "I've felt bad ever since [that] we didn't continue. All it took was a little bit of flour and pancakes, and we had lots of syrup and those kids—they were *hungry*."

It's been almost seventy years but Walden still thinks about that family and the opportunity lost to help someone. In his heart, he is still very much like the little boy who helps the old lady across the icy street.

Art, too, chose to become a teacher. In 1941, he worked in the tiny town of Monitor, east of Consort, before enlisting in the army. But just before he signed up, Art met Madeline McCallister at a young people's meeting at the church.

"Oh, look at that girl. I've got to meet her. I've got to meet her!" Art remembers saying. "That was Madeline."

Art jokes that he took her for a boat ride and "I was singing, 'I was paddlin' Madeline home!'"

Madeline, still happily married after fifty-six years, teases Art: "Isn't it wonderful to tell someone the story of your life, and they *listen?*"

There was a war on, and the Smith brothers felt they had to do their duty. Art and his brothers Lloyd, Harold, and Clarence also signed up. All began as signalmen. Lloyd became a major but the rest of them were "buck privates, all of us," says Art, who later became a gunner in the Fourth Canadian Armoured Division. Harold, Lloyd, and Clarence all joined the Royal Canadian Corps of Signals.

Art served in Belgium, Holland, and Germany, where one of his main jobs was to accept messages from a front-line observation post.

"That saved his life one time," Walden says. "He had to go run a line and when he came back, a bomb had dropped and killed his friends." Four of Art's companions were killed by an eighty-eight-millimetre artillery shell.

Art's twin brother, Harold, was stationed in Brighton, England, where he became one of the war's many casualties, although his death was due to a tragic accident rather than enemy fire. One night in January 1944, when he was putting in overtime as a signaller, he walked to the camp kitchen for coffee. There was a blackout under-way at the time, and in the darkness, Harold was run over by an army gun carrier.

Art and Clarence returned to Canada in 1946 (Lloyd had always been stationed in Canada), after which Art went to the University of Alberta for his Bachelor of Science in Agriculture and his Bachelor of Education. He and Madeline were married in 1949. He found himself a teaching job in Eckville, Alberta, and, by 1954, they settled in Wetaskiwin, where Art worked as a biology teacher. He taught at Wetaskiwin High School for the next thirty-one years.

"He used to hypnotize chickens," Walden says.

Art agrees. "I'm Alberta's number one chicken hypnotizer. I'm not kidding."

Former students still come up to him and say, "Mr. Smith, I remember you. You're the one who showed us how to hypnotize chickens."

How do you hypnotize a chicken? There's nothing to it, Art says. Just make them concentrate—the chickens, that is—make them look at your finger and concentrate.

"First you need to get your finger, chalk or whatever, right at the bird's beak, so its beady eyes are looking," says Art. Then, draw a line. When the chicken is hypnotized, it's "flaked out, lying on its side, eyes closed. The ones to easily hypnotize were young roosters— couldn't seem to do the job with an old hen."

Walden still has a teaching evaluation document he got from Sunnybrook in 1933, the first year he taught; he went on to become principal there for fourteen years, and later served as principal in the town of Winfield for twenty years. After his retirement in 1975, Walden went on to substitute teach until 1993 so he could say he had taught for sixty years.

"My philosophy is when you retire, then you've got to do something worthwhile that you couldn't do when you were on the job," Art says. He used to tell Walden that they had been teaching all their lives and now it was time to do something different.

"Diversify," Walden says, and laughs.

And diversify they did. Besides all their activities in Wetaskiwin, they also joined forces with Clarence, the baby of the family, who lived in Medicine Hat. He was the best volunteer in Alberta, Art says. Clarence organized a food bank and soup kitchen.

"He built a root cellar," Art says. "He and a minister built a root cellar and all the churches came to pick up fresh vegetables, potatoes, carrots, turnips, and cabbages. 'I don't want any tins,' Clarence would say. 'Corn Flakes—forget it! We're going to get *fresh* vegetables.'"

Clarence, with all the Smith charm, would get extra vegetables from a friend who had a warehouse, someone else who ran a market garden, and others.

"He was the only one they would give it to," says Art.

"They knew they could trust him," Walden adds. Someone less scrupulous might have tried to sell the vegetables, he implies.

The Smith charity spirit isn't confined to Alberta. In 1992, Walden and Clarence travelled to Jamaica for a holiday. But rather than just lie back and enjoy the sun, they volunteered to help build an orphanage.

Earlier, in 1990, Walden had helped fund a convoy of medical and school supplies bound for El Salvador.

"Clarence and I bought a school bus between us [for] eight thousand dollars," Walden says. "Then they took the seats out and put in donations, medical supplies among other things. They drove it all the way down [from Canada to El Salvador]."

There were about eight vehicles in the convoy, mostly old trucks.

"You can imagine the trouble they had crossing all those borders," says Walden.

Clarence went along with the convoy, but Walden and Art stayed behind.

"I should have [gone]. Every time I think back on it I wished I'd gone," Art says. He and Madeline, through the United Church, had sponsored a family from El Salvador to come to Canada in 1984.

Clarence, a veterinarian by profession, was helping others right up until the end of his life. The Canadian government sent him to China four times to teach Chinese ranchers the Canadian methods of raising beef cattle. On his last trip overseas, Clarence learned that he had prostate cancer.

Clarence died in June 2001. Over the years, the Smith family has lost two of its brothers and two sisters; it makes the bond between those remaining even stronger. By 2006, their sister Margaret, now in her nineties, and brother Lloyd, in his late eighties, were still living in British Columbia. Art and Walden try to see each other every day, which isn't difficult considering all the work they do in the community.

"The thing about Walden is he likes everybody," says Art. "He likes everybody and he likes them so well, he embarrasses his wife because everybody's welcome: 'Come on and stay overnight,' Walden would say."

Walden also wants the world to know about his kid brother.

"He's about the best brother anybody could have, the best by far," he says. "He couldn't be better. One year, I had no driver's licence. I had a seizure so they said no driving for a year. Anyway, he was over there [at our place] just about every day. 'Where do you want to go today, Wald?' That's the kind of brother he is."

Art tries to shrug it off.

"He'd do it for anybody else, too," Walden says. "He does do it for anybody else."

As the interview ends, so does this brief lull in the lives of the Smith brothers. As Walden and Art fold up the card table, someone comes to the door to pick up the bagels for a local charity. Doug will soon be calling to see when Art wants to pick up the soup from the Wayside Inn so they can take it to the church kitchen to bag and freeze it. Art's overheated car is ready to go into the shop for repairs so he can use it to drive the local man to his cancer treatments. And Art and Madeline haven't even had their supper yet.

In spite of overheating cars, inclement weather, and snarling dogs, the work must go on. There are, after all, still lots of people in Wetaskiwin who need their help.

From left, Dolores Samuel and Katherine High. How do you thank someone for the gift of a kidney? (Photo by T. J. Georgi)

Katherine High and Dolores Samuel

This is my destiny

It is a fine summer day in Edmonton as two women reunite to tell their story. There is a definite chemistry between them and an easy camaraderie. Part of this is the relaxed kinship of people who know each other well and who love each other very much, but there is something else. These two share a bond most people will never experience—a bond forged in the heat of a life-and-death decision. Their names are Dolores Samuel and Katherine High, and their story starts in 1996, when Dolores Samuel decided to take a cruise to Alaska.

If anyone deserved a break, it was Dolores.

⫸

Originally from Trinidad, Dolores Samuel arrived in Canada in 1955 and enrolled in the College of Optometry in Toronto. She fell in love with an Estevan, Saskatchewan-based dental surgeon named Philip Samuel and married him ten days after her graduation in 1959.

Dolores moved to Saskatchewan with Philip and started a family, beginning with daughter Margaret and son Stephen. In 1962 Dolores began her own optometry practice while she was expecting her third child, Thérèse. Her fourth, Valerie, was born in November 1964.

Then tragedy struck. On 30 December 1964, Philip had a massive and fatal heart attack, leaving Dolores and four children, the youngest only six weeks of age.

"Phil was fifty-one years young," says Dolores. "He died at home. He was playing chess with a friend in the kitchen and went to lie down. His speech was garbled so I called for the doctor a few blocks away, and he was gone before the doctor arrived."

Dolores now had the challenge of raising four kids alone. She stayed in Estevan until Valerie was ready to start Grade one, then moved her family to Edmonton, where she got a job in the optical department at Woodward's department store. In 1973, she started her own practice in north-central Edmonton and later opened two more practices in Edmonton and Red Deer.

By 1996, Dolores had been a single mom and an optometrist for more than thirty years. And they hadn't been easy years. Now, with her children grown, Dr. Samuel was looking forward to the Alaskan cruise.

Just before she left, Dolores noticed that her ankles were swollen, but she felt healthy. In fact, she was proud to say she'd never had an operation in her life. Swollen ankles are not that unusual, so she put it out of her mind and got ready to enjoy her trip.

The cruise to Alaska gave Dolores enough memories for a lifetime. One of her favourite moments was sitting on deck with friends the night of the summer equinox and watching the coastal mountains go by for hours, illuminated by the dimming summer sky.

But by the time Dolores returned from the cruise, her health was declining alarmingly. There was more swelling in her ankles, and her energy level plummeted.

"I came back from this cruise and I was so tired. I thought—what? I took a cruise and it was so relaxing," Dolores says.

She went to her doctor for some blood tests. The next day, she got the phone call that changed her life forever.

"Get in the hospital right away," the doctor ordered.

It was June 1996 and the beginning of a frightening journey, one Dolores Samuel never asked to take and one she wouldn't wish on anybody.

The doctor determined that Dolores's kidneys were working at a mere twenty-five per cent of their capacity. Although she knew she had high blood pressure—one possible harbinger of kidney trouble down the line—Dolores knew of no family history of kidney disease.

Her kidneys were shutting down and the doctor's first recommendation was that she go on dialysis.

"I did not want to go on dialysis—that would turn my whole life upside down!" she says. Getting a transplant was also out of the question—the idea of surgery terrified her. So she looked for an alternative.

She tried a drug called prednisone for three weeks. One of its uses is to treat kidney disorders, and it is similar to the hormone produced by the adrenal glands (which are located adjacent to the kidneys). It's also designed to relieve inflammation and swelling. But the prednisone was only a temporary solution. Dolores changed her diet and exercise regimen and sought the advice of a renal dietician. She even consulted a Buddhist monk/medical practitioner, who prescribed special herbal preparations and exercises.

Dolores also made a difficult decision about her career. She couldn't fight kidney disease and maintain not one, but three optometry practices (one of them a ninety-minute drive away in Red Deer). Her health had to come first, so she decided to close down her practice and retire in her early sixties.

"I was forced into retirement. I was not ready to retire," she says.

Dolores sold her home in Edmonton during the summer of 1997 and bought a retirement condo overlooking the sea in Trinidad. Her plan was to spend the winter in her native country, and she moved into an apartment in Edmonton in order to spend the summers there close to her family.

With these changes, plus effective use of high blood pressure medication, Dolores kept her condition under control for the next five years, but she knew this was just delaying the inevitable. By 2001, her condition had worsened to the point where she had no choice but to go on dialysis.

Dolores was determined that kidney failure would not change her life drastically. She would adapt to her new circumstances with the same gritty perseverance that saw her raise four children alone and build up a successful practice.

She looked at the dialysis options available to her and decided to undertake peritoneal dialysis. This requires no heavy machines; instead, a tube and catheter are surgically inserted into the abdomen and the patient can make the exchange of dialysis fluid every four to six hours.

The other alternative, hemodialysis, is the method most commonly associated with dialysis. It requires a large artificial kidney machine to cleanse the blood of the toxins and waste that a normal kidney would filter.

Peritoneal dialysis cleaned the blood inside her body instead of in a machine, so she didn't require constant hospital visits, and the machinery involved was portable enough that Dolores could travel, including to her beloved Trinidad.

To lighten her mood, she named her portable overnight machine "Josephine" and the catheter "Charlie." Airline personnel were helpful, letting her travel with Josephine without extra cost and giving Dolores passes to the business class lounge so she could do her exchanges.

A specially designed Samsonite carry-on bag contained her equipment. It held two dialysis pouches in a heated tray powered by a plug-in device. A separate, collapsible pole to support the dialysis bag during exchanges completed the kit. The kit was portable enough that Dolores could do the exchange in an airport washroom or even at a rest stop during a camping trip.

Still, it wasn't a perfect solution. After swimming in the sea in Trinidad one day, she contracted peritonitis, an inflammation of the membrane lining the cavity of the abdomen. Doctors believed the infection began in the exit site of the catheter in her abdomen, even after Dolores took the recommended precautions, which included applying a special ointment to the entrance site. Dolores eventually had to have an operation to replace the old catheter and tube.

"After that incident, I never swam in the sea again, just waded and splashed water on my body," Dolores says.

Like the medication, dialysis was ultimately a band-aid solution. Dolores knew an even greater life-or-death challenge lay ahead.

"You know, dialysis is only a stepping stone to transplant," the doctor told Dolores.

"At that point I didn't want to hear it," Dolores recalls. "I did not want to consider transplant—that would butcher up my body. I'd never, ever had an operation in my life, not even for tonsillitis."

But fate was about to step in. One day in the hospital, Dolores saw a man playing with his grandson. He told her he was seventy-two years old and had recently had a kidney transplant.

"And I thought, what's good for the goose is good for the gander. If he can have a transplant, why can't *I* have a transplant?" she says.

———

There are three kinds of kidney donors. The first is a recently deceased donor, known as a cadaver donor. A living donor transplant, on the other hand, involves a live person whose blood and tissue type are a match to those of the recipient. Brothers and sisters are usually the best matches, but another relative could also be a match. Far less common is the live unrelated donor, a person not genetically related to the recipient but who nonetheless has matching blood and tissue types. Live donor transplants have a better success rate—ninety to ninety-five per cent in the first year—than cadavers, and these transplanted kidneys last an average of fifteen to twenty years, which is also longer than the average for cadaver kidneys.

A search in Dolores's family failed to find a suitable donor. Dolores put her name on the waiting list for a cadaver kidney. Now she could only wait and pray.

Her lifestyle was soon impacted. During the winter of 2002–2003, Dolores travelled to Trinidad and discovered upon her return to Edmonton that she had been taken off the transplant waiting list because she would have been too far away from Edmonton to return in time for a cadaver transplant had one become available. Once back in Alberta, she had to start almost at the bottom of the list again. As long as the spectre of a transplant remained, one of Dolores' joys—travel—would be denied her.

———

The second hero in our story enters the picture around Easter Sunday 2003. By this time, Dolores Samuel was running out of options. Her daughter, Thérèse, had watched her mother go through kidney failure, dialysis, and now the awful anticipation of waiting for someone to die in order to get a new lease on life. During this difficult time, Thérèse often confided in one of her oldest friends, Katherine High.

Katherine first met Thérèse in 1977 when they were in Grade ten together at Archbishop MacDonald Catholic High School in the west end of Edmonton. Their birthdays were only four days apart—Katherine was one year and four days older than Thérèse—and they became constant companions. Katherine, whose parents separated a couple of weeks before her sixteenth birthday, came to be treated as a member of the Samuel family and the two girls enjoyed frequent sleepovers. She also spent many Christmases with the Samuels. When she later had two children at a young age, it was Thérèse and Dolores who were always there to support her.

"They always included me in everything," Katherine recalls. "I was Thérèse's friend and sister, and then the whole family basically adopted me. Of course, I wouldn't go away, that's why," she laughs. By 2003, Katherine and Thérèse were both past forty years of age, but they still enjoyed one of those rare friendships that last a lifetime.

One day, out of the blue and perhaps out of desperation, Thérèse asked Katherine a strange question.

"Do you have O-positive blood and an extra kidney?"

Thérèse still remembers Katherine's answer. "She said, 'Yeah, I've got type O-positive. I'd give your mom a kidney.' No hesitation."

Thérèse could hardly believe what she was hearing but wasted no time in calling her mother. It would be the most important message of Dolores's life.

"Mom, Kathy wants to give you a kidney," she said.

In 2004, the Capital Health Region (which includes Edmonton) conducted seventy kidney transplants; of this number, thirty-six were cadaveric kidneys, twenty-three were kidneys from living related donors, and only eleven were from living unrelated donors. One of these eleven would come from Katherine High.

Katherine would discover first-hand that there's much more to donating a kidney than simply having the same blood type and undergoing an operation. It isn't as quick and easy as it is in the movies. In real life, Katherine would face a year of tests before the operation could proceed. But she was determined to do this for the adopted mom she called "Gramsie."

"I never actually really thought about it," Katherine says. "These were the tests I had to do, so I just did them."

Even the Samuels, who knew her well, didn't know what kind of determination Katherine really had. They were about to find out.

It would turn out to be one of the most eventful years in Katherine's life. Not long before she started the tests to see if her kidney was compatible she met someone and fell in love.

Katherine's twenty-year-old son Geoff had been living in an apartment on Edmonton's west side when there was a massive fire. After the blaze, Geoff was allowed back in to salvage any belongings from the wreckage.

"When I was over there helping him to clean up and everything, I ran into this big guy," recalls Katherine.

"Think teddy bear," Thérèse pipes in.

Katherine was in the kitchen of the burned apartment when she heard her son talking to someone. There was no electricity in the suite but they'd hooked up a stereo outside in the parking lot. Katherine heard a booming voice and thought that whoever was talking to Geoff was just trying to be heard above the stereo, so she went out and turned it down. The stranger stared at her.

"His infamous words were, 'Who the hell are you?'" Katherine remembers with a smile. "I said, 'I'm his mom.'"

Katherine was more than a little intrigued with Michael High, who was working as a handyman at the time. The two of them each found out that the other was single and a serious romance followed almost immediately. The couple planned to marry.

But then Katherine found herself considering another life-changing commitment. How would Michael feel about the love of his life donating one of her kidneys?

"He was always supportive," she says. "We had to make a decision."

Mike didn't have children of his own. If they were going to have a child together, they had to decide soon. "I met him when I was forty and married when I was forty-one," Katherine says. "Because of our ages, it was something that would have to be decided on immediately.

"When I inquired with the living donor program, I was told that if I became pregnant I would have to wait approximately a year-and-a-half before I was able to donate as I would have to recover from the pregnancy [first]. They did tell me that in no way would the surgery affect my ability to become pregnant after, but I knew that we were looking at an extensive time delay, and by then I would be almost forty-three before I could become pregnant.

"I had to decide: give birth to another child or give birth to a kidney," Katherine says. "[Do] we delay Dolores's only chance at that time for a pain-free, normal life, or do we go ahead with the donation and give up our dream of having a child? In the end, there was no question what the choice would be. I think I made the right choice."

Katherine went ahead with the testing, feeling secure that her fiancé and her son, Geoff, were satisfied that she knew what she was doing.

On top of all this, Katherine also had to balance her commitment to Dolores with feelings of sadness. The same month she agreed to the transplant, she learned that her first son, Stephen, had passed away. She had given birth to Stephen when she was just a teenager and had given the boy up for adoption. She began searching for him on his twenty-fourth birthday, and she finally located him—one month after his death. But there was some joy in this when she learned that Stephen had a son (in August 2004 she would meet her grandson for the first time).

In the days after Katherine made her promise, Dolores didn't hear from Katherine for awhile and wondered if someone in her family might have objected to the transplant.

"I didn't want to push," Dolores says. She wanted Katherine to be at peace with her decision.

At one point she told Katherine, "If you want to back out, just go ahead and back out." But Katherine was surprised Dolores would ever think she wouldn't go through with it.

There is emotional and mental trauma to losing a part of one's body, even if by choice. For this reason, the very first step in Katherine's testing process was a three-hour session with a psychologist to make absolutely sure she knew what she was doing, and that she was doing it willingly.

Katherine continued with medical tests through the spring of 2003, all the while making plans for her wedding.

Katherine and Mike were married on 14 June 2003. It was a Saturday, and she and Dolores were scheduled to appear at the University of Alberta Hospital for a special blood mixing test very early on the Monday morning. They both had to be present—the blood needed to be fresh so doctors could see if their tissue types were compatible and that there would be no surprises during the transplant.

"If her blood had reacted to mine, then that's it, they [wouldn't] go any further," Katherine says.

One of Mike and Katherine's wedding presents was a night at the Fantasyland Hotel at West Edmonton Mall for the night before Katherine and Dolores's scheduled test. Katherine would have to leave her new husband around 7 AM on Monday in order to get to the hospital in time for the test.

As it turned out, Dolores woke that Monday with a bad backache and had to cancel the appointment. What she didn't know at the time was that the hospital wasn't able to contact Katherine, and that Katherine showed up right on time. The test was rescheduled for two weeks later.

As if this weren't enough, Katherine had her own personal health scare to deal with in the midst of the new marriage and the tests. Just after her wedding, doctors found a tumour on her thyroid.

"I had two options," she says. "Surgery would further delay the testing for the transplant as I had already had to put them on hold until the tumour was dealt with. Or I could opt for radioactive iodine."

Katherine chose the iodine and began treatment in September 2003. She would have to wait three months before they could tell if the tumour was gone. This was frustrating for Katherine, since she knew that Dolores couldn't afford to wait much longer for the transplant.

Dolores was more concerned about Katherine than about her own condition.

"Once Katherine started testing for the donor process, I was taken off the cadaver list [as a] routine procedure," she says. "After the tumor was detected on her thyroid gland, I wondered about going on the donor list again. My concern then was whether Katherine, or her family, may have been getting a bit frustrated and tired of the whole issue. Once I determined that she was okay with it, I was okay, too.

"Other than the constant concern about Katherine, my mood was mainly one of excitement, always focused on getting back into that beautiful blue Caribbean Sea."

As if her life wasn't complicated enough, fate would toss still another curve ball at Katherine near the end of 2003, just as she was about to go to the hospital to find out the status of the tumour. On 14 December Mike collapsed and was sent to the hospital where he was diagnosed with an abnormal heart rhythm. He was sent home, though he was required to return for a short hospital stay after Christmas.

Finally, in February 2004, Katherine got a clean bill of health after successful treatment of the tumour, which turned out to be benign. The tests for the kidney transplant, on hold since the previous autumn, could now resume.

In April 2004, a year of waiting, delays, and tests came to an end with the best possible outcome.

"Dolores and I were told that the transplant would take place on May 4," Katherine recalls. "I was elated and frightened at the same time. What if, after all this, the operation would not be a success? I don't think I could have handled that very well."

Dolores was relieved that they were finally declared a match.

"I felt really good but I was always concerned about Kathy," she says.

Before the day of the surgery, Katherine and Dolores discussed what was about to happen to the two of them.

"I can't really believe you're doing this," Dolores told her. She would never forget Katherine's answer: "I always wanted to be part of your family, anyway, so now you're stuck with me for life."

Thérèse would see each of them to the doors of the operating room.

"I think it was the day before that I realized, this is my best friend that I've known for [twenty-seven] years, and my mom, and they're both having major surgery," Thérèse recalls. "I hadn't taken into account that there was going to be these two people—that are so special to me—in surgery."

Before leaving for the operating room, Katherine handed Thérèse her rosary and said, "This is my destiny." These are words Thérèse will never forget.

Once her mom and her best friend were in the operating room,

Thérèse was suddenly entirely alone. "I went back and prayed the whole time the surgeries were happening," she says.

Both women had been briefed about the procedure. Katherine's left kidney would be removed, preserved in ice, and placed in Dolores's body. Unless the failing kidneys are diseased, they are usually not removed as the new kidney is placed in the recipient's lower abdomen. Dolores would now have three kidneys, but only her "second-hand kidney" would do the work. By this time, her kidneys had almost completely shut down

One aspect of the surgery caused Katherine some discomfort after the fact.

"In order to get to the kidney, they have to bend you like a pretzel," she recalls. "Because of where the kidney is positioned they have to drop your legs and your arms so it's easier to get to the kidney."

Katherine had had a bad back since she was a teenager. The "pretzel" position caused her pain. She remembers feeling it even before she came out of the anaesthetic.

"The first thing I felt even before I was fully awake was my back," she says. It hurt more than the incision site. And that wasn't all. "Sometimes they have to snip the rib or the cartilage. In my case they snipped the cartilage. That was the most painful part of it." There was also a minor complication for Katherine when doctors discovered she had an extra artery leading into the kidney.

Finally, after eight hours—three hours for Katherine to remove the kidney, and another five for Dolores in order to implant it—the operation was over.

Dolores was still groggy when the surgeon, Dr. Ron Moore, came in to check on her.

"Who are you?" Dolores asked.

"I'm Bob the Plumber," he told her, straight-faced.

Katherine remembers the doctor had "a little twinkle in his eye." Even through her pain, Katherine recognized a kindred spirit who liked to laugh.

Dolores and Katherine were on the same floor of the hospital but still far apart. Each wanted to see how the other was doing. Katherine was helped into a wheelchair and made the agonizing journey, driven by Thérèse, down the hallways. Even her snail's pace was way too fast.

"When [she] wheeled me across, every bump was 'Oh, geez!'" Katherine remembers.

Once in Dolores's room, the two were too battle-weary for emotion. That would come later.

"We just basically looked at each other and thought, 'Okay, we're both doing okay, so—goin' back to bed now,'" Katherine says.

After a transplant, there are usually a few tense days as doctors closely monitor the relocated kidney for any signs of rejection. That's when "Gramsie" and her "adopted" daughter found out that not only their hearts matched, their kidneys did, too.

Katherine was now, quite literally, a part of the family.

A few weeks after the operation, Dolores and Katherine were both recovering nicely. Dolores's brother was visiting and so Dolores decided to invite Katherine and Mike for supper. Dolores spoke to a local bakery and asked them to make a special cake for the occasion.

They laughed after they heard her request, Dolores recalls. They told her, "We never got a request like this before."

"I said, 'You probably never will again.'"

Katherine had named "their" kidney Sidney. So the cake read "Farewell—SIDNEY—Welcome," describing Sidney the kidney's journey from Katherine's body into Dolores's. "And then they iced a lovely kidney beside it," Dolores says, delighted.

The doctors had warned the two patients that it would take six months to a year for their bodies to fully recover from the surgery.

"Now I can't die. I've got to take good care of myself for Kathy," says Dolores.

The effect of the surgery on both women was remarkable. A year later, they looked ten years younger than they actually were. Dolores's life would never be the way it was before that cruise in 1996. She would have to take anti-rejection drugs for the rest of her life, and she would also have to continue to watch her diet, as she had when she was on dialysis, but at least she was allowed to once again eat treats like chocolate, pecans, bananas, and oranges—items that had been forbidden under her dialysis diet.

And best of all, Dolores was able to retire Josephine, the portable overnight dialysis machine that she had to take with her everywhere. Dolores was able to enjoy her retirement winters in Trinidad to the fullest, and not long after the surgery she became a great-grandmother for the second time when her grandchild, Kerri, had a son.

"She's got her life back, that's the thing," Katherine says.

Katherine's life also changed. With one remaining kidney, Katherine faced no dietary restrictions but she was now required to monitor her blood pressure regularly, since the kidneys regulate blood pressure and any changes can be one of the first signs that something is wrong.

The doctor also warned Katherine against "jumping out of planes or bungee jumping or motorcycling." He was only partly joking. Contact sports and risky activities like skydiving are not encouraged for someone with a single kidney, for fear that the remaining organ could be damaged.

"Scuba diving, I guess, is out. I've always wanted to do that. Seriously," Katherine says.

Thoughts of scuba diving, or perhaps snorkelling, remind Katherine and Dolores of Trinidad. Katherine would like to go one day but there's a hitch. The woman who gave up a kidney is deathly afraid of flying.

"I've never flown," Katherine says. When her family moved from Montreal to Alberta when she was young, half the family took the plane while Katherine, her father, and one brother drove all the way.

"Now this is the neat thing," Thérèse adds. "Her kidney has flown to Trinidad. She's going one piece at a time."

"Yeah, and I'm not following," Katherine retorts.

Why did Katherine do it? She didn't have to. Dolores would have understood, whatever her decision. Donating a kidney isn't the easiest way to start a marriage, plus there were all the other complications—learning the whereabouts her of long-lost (and, sadly, deceased) son, her own health crisis and that of her husband, as well as her own concerns about the operation.

"I love [Dolores] and she needed it," Katherine says. "My dad died when I was twenty-one. At my dad's funeral when we were at the cemetery and I was crying and [Dolores] came over and just held me. And my mom actually came over and I kind of pushed my mom away."

But she welcomed Dolores's hug, and her love.

"I never forgot that," Katherine says.

Here was a woman Katherine deeply admired, a woman who'd raised four children on her own since the youngest was six weeks old. Even with all her responsibilities, "she accepted me into the family years ago and has always made me feel welcome and loved. I was thankful for the opportunity to be able to help her in this way," Katherine says.

Dolores admits there is no way to thank someone for giving up a kidney.

"There's no way I can thank her. How can you thank her?" she asks. "There are still some lovely people in this world—some selfless people in this world who will give up a vital organ to save somebody else's life."

Katherine has a message for someone who might be in a position to donate a kidney: "It's scary. It hurts for awhile. But it's the best thing I've ever done in my life." She pauses for a few moments. "And if I had to do it again tomorrow, I would."

After her experience, Dolores Samuel wrote a poem commemorating the event:

An Angel for Life
It was eight years ago that I got the call,
"Your lab test, my dear, tells it all,
Your kidneys have gone on strike," they say—
NO WAY, NO WAY, NO WAY, JOSE!

I wouldn't believe this could happen to me,
I've always been so healthy, you see.
Never anything more than a cold,
Blood pressure a bit high I had long been told.

For five years I toyed with exercise and diet,
At first everything remained so quiet.
"I'll beat this thing," I said. "You'll see"
And basked in a false sense of security.

So I worked and travelled and lived my life,
And all went smoothly without any strife.
Five years passed by and then suddenly,
The whole world collapsed—dialysis for me!

Time to slow down and give up the pace,
I had to admit I had lost the race.
"What next?" I asked. "To continue I can't.
The next step must be a kidney transplant."

One day I saw a man of seventy-two,
Enjoying his transplant—his grandson, too.
What's good for the goose is good for the gander,
So I made up my mind, no time to wonder.

I prayed for a donor and sat back to wait,
And see what the Lord had planned for my Fate.
Two years went by and on one Easter Sunday,
A glimmer of Hope seemed to transcend my way.

An Angel appeared in the form of Katherine,
She offered me a kidney, as her 'surrogate' kin.
My own kids couldn't help so she vowed to try,
A school friend of my daughter's from days gone by.

Our blood types matched, that we knew for sure,
Would it all be a match now we've opened the door?
The tests were all started with great trepidation,
It took a whole year—but oh! What elation!

The end of the story, I'm happy to say,
Came to pass on the fourth of the month of May.
Two thousand and four the year it came to be,
That Sidney the Kidney passed from Katherine to me.

Now I can eat whatever I please,
Chocolates, nuts, ice cream, and peas.
I can go on vacation and swim in the sea,
Who would think this ever would come back for me.

Katherine, you're an angel from the Sky,
No way can I thank you, I won't even try.
Take good care of her, Dear God up above,
I leave her with you, with all of my Love.

(Dr. Dolores Samuel, O.D., 16 September 2004)

Sources

Charlie and Winnie Ellis

Ellis Bird Farm newsletter, Myrna Pearman, ed. Vol. 18, No. 2, Fall/Winter 2004.

Shantz, Bryan R. "Bluebird Country." *Omphalos Magazine.* Vol. 2, No. 1, Spring 1986.

website: www.ellisbirdfarm.ab.ca

Jude Fine

Senior Dog Rescue Society website: www.seniordogrescue.org

Dave Irvine-Halliday

Bondar, Roberta. *Touching the Earth.* Toronto: Key Porter Books, 1995.

Chandler, Graham. "David Irvine-Halliday: Founder, Light Up the World." *Imperial Oil Review.* Vol. 87, No. 448, 2003.

Munday, Bonnie. *Reader's Digest Hero of the Year: Giving Light, Spreading Hope.* www.readersdigest.ca, July 2004.

"Press Release: 2002 Rolex Laureate Returns to Calgary." Calgary: www.eng.ucalgary.ca, 28 October 2002.

"Press Release: Reader's Digest Canadian Hero of the Year 2004." Montreal: www.readersdigest.ca, 14 June 2004.

website: www.lutw.org

Jeff Liberty

D'Amour, Mike. "Gold Medal Rescue: Olympic Diver Saves Woman from Icy River." Calgary: *Calgary Sun*, 13 November 2001.

Smith, Peter. "Brave Action Recognized." Calgary: *Calgary Sun*, 16 November 2001.

Ron Lyle

Fleming, Freeda, and Angie Edgerton, eds. *The Days Before Yesterday: History of Rocky Mountain House District.* Rocky Mountain House: Rocky Mountain House Reunion Historical Society, 1977.

Land, Forest, Wildlife. Edmonton: Department of Lands and Forests, Natural Resources, Vol. 8, No. 4, Winter 1965–66.

Barb Tarbox

Barb Tarbox. Edmonton: Alberta Alcohol and Drug Abuse Commission, http://tobacco.aadac.com/media_campaigns/barb_tarbox/, 12 April 2005.

Staples, David. *Barb's Miracle.* Edmonton: River Books, 2004.

Index

About Fifth House

Fifth House Publishers, a Fitzhenry & Whiteside company, is a proudly western- Canadian press. Our publishing specialty is non-fiction as we believe that every community must possess a positive understanding of its worth and place if it is to remain vital and progressive. Fifth House is committed to "bringing the West to the rest" by publishing approximately twenty books a year about the land and people who make this region unique. Our books are selected for their quality and contribution to the understanding of western-Canadian (and Canadian) history, culture, and environment.

Alberta Originals: Stories of Albertans Who Made a Difference,
Brian Brennan

Boondoggles, Bonanzas, and Other Alberta Stories,
Brian Brennan

Building a Province: 60 Alberta Lives, Brian Brennan

Gateway City: Stories from Edmonton's Past, Alex Mair

It Happened in Manitoba: Stories of the Red River Province,
Don Aiken

Looking Back: True Tales from Saskatchewan's Past,
Paul Dederick and Bill Waiser

Romancing the Rockies: Mountaineers, Missionaries, Marilyn, and More, Brian Brennan

Saskatchewan's Own: People Who Made a Difference,
Verne Clemence

Scoundrels and Scallywags: Characters from Alberta's Past,
Brian Brennan

Where the River Runs: Stories of the Saskatchewan and the People Drawn to Its Shores, Victor Carl Friesen